Legacy
of an Ordinary *Woman*

L. J. SHOOK

BALBOA.PRESS
A DIVISION OF HAY HOUSE

Balboa Press books may be ordered through booksellers or by contacting:

Balboa Press
A Division of Hay House
1663 Liberty Drive
Bloomington, IN 47403
www.balboapress.com
844-682-1282

Because of the dynamic nature of the Internet, any web addresses or
links contained in this book may have changed since publication and
may no longer be valid. The views expressed in this work are solely those
of the author and do not necessarily reflect the views of the publisher,
and the publisher hereby disclaims any responsibility for them.

The author of this book does not dispense medical advice or prescribe the use
of any technique as a form of treatment for physical, emotional, or medical
problems without the advice of a physician, either directly or indirectly. The
intent of the author is only to offer information of a general nature to help
you in your quest for emotional and spiritual well-being. In the event you use
any of the information in this book for yourself, which is your constitutional
right, the author and the publisher assume no responsibility for your actions.

Print information available on the last page.

ISBN: 979-8-7652-5592-6 (sc)
ISBN: 979-8-7652-5591-9 (e)

Balboa Press rev. date: 10/28/2024

Contents

A Diamond Cutter 1

A Few More Times..5

A Friend's Prayer 6

A Little Christmas Shopping 7

A Remarkable Thing Happened 11

A Special Brand of "Fishin"...12

A Survival Guide for Grandma 16

A Whopping Fish Tale...23

Answered Prayer..25

Back off Angel..28

Because I Can..31

Bent Lips 37

Bertha..38

Big City Beat...41

Big Shift..44

Bush Whacked..48

Catcher of Dreams..51

Courage...55

Dare to Be All You Can Be 59

Dare to Be..63

Ebony Man, Black Sister, My Friend.........................64

Eeegads Fifty-Three!!..66

Expectation!!!..70

Family Thorn...72

Family Thorn...76

Fingerprints We Leave...77

Flat Stanley And Kolton...82

Fried Egg Brain..83

Gather Together...86

Gittin' Her Wind..87

Grammy This is Commando!...88

Grandma Was No Ordinary Woman......................................92
Hard Day of Dying..96
Here Fishy, Fishy...Here Fishy, Fishy 101
Horse Fly on A String...103
How Granny Scared the FBI 105
How Well Does Your Attitude Serve You? 108
I Miss...113
Imaginary Lover..115
Kissed By an Angel...117
Lift us Father..120
Modern Man 121
My Dear Joe..122
My Father's Garage...123
My Right!...126
New Boots for Carla..127
Old Age Birthday Poem 129
Old Tree New Branches..130
Old Woman's Cart...133
Open Heart Surgery 135
Picket Fence...143
Radio Man 146
Raindrops Keep Falling on Your Head 149
Rough Diamond 151
Run, Me Maw, Run..152
Rylee, Happy First 2013...155
Santa's Letter for Martha..156
Settled In and Unsettled..157
Seventy and Six 161
Showdown at Register Three 165
Small and Simple Challenges 169
Sometimes You Get It Right 173
Sun Kitty..176
The Alley Cat..178
The Greatest of These Is Love...181

The Hands That Lifted Charlie 182
Third Shift Blues...184
Toad Kissing 185
Tood and Luke 187
Twinkle of Color 190
What a Difference a Dream Can Make.............................. 191
When I'm an Ole' Woman... 196
When The Music Ends.. 198
Writer's Block 205
You Have Loved Well Poem.. 206

A Diamond Cutter

By L. J. Shook

We can say we are irritated, confused, hurt and intrigued by them, sometimes all at the same time, but people are still the best show going on around us. My friends and family can contest the fact that I love to go off by myself for long periods of time and totally avoid people. The writer in me needs quiet, uninterrupted time to contemplate the people that I have met. I sort through their character and replay the script of their last life production they have played out. It is a lot like panning for gold in a creek bed, sifting endless pieces of human behavior through a strainer until a colorful or valuable nugget is found.

We are all made up of a million little pieces of DNA from the world's gene pool. None of us are without value, and it is the arrangement of these million little pieces that make us unique and flawed. Every good writer knows that you can't have a life-story without conflict thrown in to stir up emotions and rattle the soul to see how a person will act out the drama of their selected lives.

Spiritual grugrus tell us if we aren't living a conscious life, our auto-pilot system kicks in and a scenario from our sub-consciousness is played out for us to live. The moral is, "If you don't like your life then choose something on a conscious level." I am amazed at how many people are walking around living their lives from autopilot like a zombie movie trailer we have watched on TV, and then these people complain about the life they are living and their destination.

Even worse... making choices that emotionally and physically hurt their life and the lives of others because they don't understand the beauty and the responsibility or the divinity they have been given.

I used to be one of those people that wanted...needed to try and fix all those poor mixed-up souls around me. I could help them be better people, help their lives be happier and sane if only they would let me. If I concentrated on them then I didn't have to look at myself. My level of frustration was high, and irritation was a double-edged sword that cut both ways. There is a fine line between helping people and fixing people. It was only after I became an observer and not a fixer that I truly learned to love people with all their flaws and golden nuggets of humanity. What I learned was that unconditional love was the best fix of all.

It became apparent that the only person I had any control over was myself and even that was a risky business. When this lesson was learned the easier it became to love the people I encountered, because I finally had learned to love my imperfect and flawed self.

Watching people is the best reality show in town and it doesn't have to be manufactured on a deserted island with pre-selected characters playing survival games for artificial entertainment. Real people with real survival needs are in your backyard, at the supermarket, on the street corner and maybe in the house next door and most importantly in your house.

I have worked lots of different jobs but the one that affected me the most was working for a hospice and as a health care aide. This kind of work took me to ground zero where people behaved at their most honest and vulnerable level, in their own home and under difficult circumstances, a reality show that was truly real.

We are all connected, one to the other, whether we admit it or even want to believe it. When we pretend to be someone different than who we really are, it diminishes us all. When a person is their true authentic self or an original, we are inspired and uplifted to a higher level of consciousness and the evidence of that is felt by everyone around us.

While working for Hospice, one night I had to pull an all-night vigil for a patient with cancer. Her rail thin body and face were sunken and distorted by pain and suffering. My mind tried to imagine her true looks and personality before she had been ravaged by disease. Curious eyes searched the walls and dresser tops for pictures that would give me an idea of her true self. I needed to have a glimpse of her younger years to help complete the picture of her life. It felt out of balance seeing the dying but none of her living. She was only one of many patients that I would never know the beginning or middle of their life... only the end. I loved her as if we had been acquainted for years instead of a few short weeks. She was vulnerable, authentic, with no facade or time for pretense. Her days on this earth were in limited numbers and there was no time for anything but honest connections to the people around her. She was real and we were connected not by blood, family, familiarity, or proximity but by the bond that we call life.

I watched her son, who was married with grown children of his own, lay down on his mother's hospital bed and cradled her in his arms and give love and comfort in the only way he knew. Probably a lesson he had learned from the same mother he now held close.

Caring for a sick relative or friend requires sacrifice and dedication. The reality of death pulls us out of our illusions and forces us to be the true person that we are because there isn't any time for anything else.

I have had the privilege of seeing a thirty-eight-year-old son in the final stages of Aids, weakly crawl into his mother's bed in the wee hours of morning seeking the same comfort and reassurance he sought as a child, only this time it was about his dying instead of living.

I have felt the tug of my heart when a three-year old girl, with long blond hair and blue eyes of childhood innocence instinctively slipped her fingers through the hospital bed rails and into her beloved grandmother's hand during the final hours of her grandmother's life.

These acts are true heart to heart reality. When you have felt the pull of this kind of reality there is no going back to the pretend, prefab version of reality the world portrays. Once you understand the interdependence we have for one another and every living thing in this world you will then feel cheated going back to the false acts of dependence and separation that have been used for hundreds of years to justify pollution, prejudice, violence and intimidation.

When you hear words of truth or have a unique and believable life experience, you know and feel their truth deep in your being. We all have, at least once, felt the excitement of our spirit when encountering an original soul whose very presence lifted us up just by their proximity.

Life is a gift, given to us to use in whatever way we want. Dare to be original and lift the world. Strive to be more and don't throw away your uniqueness by being less for the comfort of fitting in or trying to obtain love that is conditional and flawed.

Always remember that the people around you are not rocks to be tossed aside or hammered into shape but rather diamonds in the rough and with just the right touch can be formed into true beauty and value. Be a diamond cutter and not a sledgehammer.

Rejoice in the diversity of the million little pieces we call people, for they are the other part of you, and you are the other part of them.

People are life and our true reality.

A Few More Times

By L. J. Shook

My life could be summed up in three easy ways.
The first nineteen years in my parent's house.
Then the next eighteen I was someone's spouse.
And the last four decades have been my freedom days.
These all blend together and have become my stay.

I am one of few that bask in the ease of my own ways,
Without always longing for a man and the marriage cage,
Decisions are now guided by spirit and not those of a wife,
It's not always easy... but free... and blissful without male strife.

The memories come from the good, not the sad.
A smile lingers and long-a-go thoughts make me glad.
Sometimes I do miss the smell of a freshly shaven man.
And the feeling on my back of a strong male's guiding hand.

A walk in the store takes me down the aisles of colorful men's shirts,
And cuffs brush my hand as I walk by, deep inside something hurts.
Oh, how I miss the long slow kiss of male lips against mine.
The right kiss that causes a glow and stars to shine.

A deep male voice still creates tremors along my spine,
Remembered long slow kisses and breathing that climb.
Thoughts of a male body pressed hard against mine,
And passion's flow that's only a matter of time.

These are my forever memories, all from my past.
Longevity of a relationship or the mind doesn't always last,
Even an old chick like me, who's a shadow of her prime,
Can still dream of a heart-pounding kiss and smile one more time.

A Friend's Prayer

My dear heavenly Father I write this little Prayer,
for the sake of my friends and all their woes and cares.

I pray you lift their hearts and fill them with light.
Lessen their yoke of living so it doesn't fit so tight.

Help them to remember the touch of a baby's hand,
And protect them in their trials across this harsh land.

Life is very trying and sometimes they lose sight,
Of the many blessings of love that shine so bright.

Help them see your creative plans,
from eternity to a single grain of sand.

Quiet their minds so their hearts will always hear,
The love you whisper softly into their waiting ear.

Bless friends with time to ponder and to do a good deed.
There are so many friends...with so many needs.

Thank you Father for listening to my simple prayer,
And all my heart-felt thoughts, just because I care.

By L.J. Shook

A Little Christmas Shopping

By L. J. Shook

    Pushing through the doors of the shopping mall brought a rush of warm air and a view of large silver and gold discount signs, heralding shoppers like a Pied Piper. The signs gently move in the artificial breeze as if waving a welcoming hand. Two seasoned shoppers like my long-time friend and I head for the sale racks like computerized guided missiles. There is nothing better than a reason to shop with an unexpected sale thrown in the bargain.

    We walk around the glimmering store like little children seeing a new toy for the first time. Big City shopping is such a joy for small town women at Christmas. Familiar holiday songs lift our spirit while festive decorations abound. My friend wandered off in search of a gift for her daughter when a rack of glitzy tops caught my eye.

    Deep in concentration I barely noticed the bump against my arm and without taking my eyes from the bargain in hand, I moved to the side to let the other shopper pass. Without warning, a hand firmly grabs my backside.

    The shock caused me to lurch forward into the rack of clothes, my brain whirls. Reality and anger slowly set in as I turn to give a piece of my mind, to the person who thinks it is okay to take liberties with my posterior. All I could see is a man with brown hair walking away, wearing a black jacket and dark pants. The slimy character never once turned around or slowed his pace.

    I stand fixed unable to move while I watch him thread his way through the store straight for my friend. Suddenly his intention clicks in my brain, I take off in a hurry to warn her. Before I can get close enough to help, I see her jump into a rack of clothes in a familiar fashion. Mr. Hand struck again. The look on her face was priceless. When I was close enough to my friend I ask, "Did you find a new way of trying on clothes?" We both gave a nervous giggle like a couple of teenagers.

With a look of indignation in her eyes she said, "Did he get you too?" I nodded and looked over to see if I could spot our groper, he was busy weaving his way to another shopper across the store. I poked my friend and we both looked in his direction, just in time to see him grope another unsuspecting female, as we watched in stunned silence.

My best friend and I exchanged, "The Look," as he walked away like nothing had happened. I said, "That was the third woman he groped in a matter of minutes and not one of us said a word because of his surprise method of attack."

I asked my friend, "Do you want to get him back?"

She answered, "You bet I do!"

The need to shop fell away replaced by the excitement of the chase. Like two military generals we plotted our battle plan. Our strategy was to circle our prey; my friend was to go one way while I go the other. When we spotted the offender, we would move in for the kill. Our thought was to come up behind him and grab his rump on both sides and give him a good dose of his own medicine.

I tried to keep my friend's red top in sight as I crept along the racks of clothes. It was hard to keep her in view because she was stalking our prey with the moves of a super-hero and crime-fighter, like her grandson had shown her.

My view was limited by hanging decorations, finally I caught sight of a red top standing a short distance away from a man with a dark jacket and pants. It looked like my friend had found him and was waiting for me. I hurried to take my position. I did not want to miss my window of opportunity to get this sleazy creep good and proper.

I rounded a circular rack of clothes tagged 50% off. With

Super Woman control I try to keep my focus. Putting my foot inside the clothes rack brought me closer to the jerk that groped women. Sliding into the center of the rack gave me a better advantage point. A hanger jabbed my ear and caught my hair. I would fit better in this space if I were my ten-year-old grandson instead of Super Avenger Grandma with wide hips.

Through gaps in the clothes, I spot our prey, and he is coming into range. The red top moved in closer. All I can make out are little bits and pieces of people through the tiny slits of space. Pushing my hand through fake designer blouses I am ready. When the red top moved alongside the dark pants, I make my move. My hand shot out from between the clothes, and I grabbed a big section of black trousers. It did not feel like a posterior, so I grabbed it again to make sure I had a good grip on the enemy. I wanted to guarantee he was going to get his Just Rewards. Suddenly the pants move and start to grow in my hand.

A loud scream causes me to let go and fall outside the clothes rack. I am not sure which was louder, my scream or the shriek of the wife belonging to the black pants that alerted the attention of every shopper in the store. The enraged wife descended on me like a robin after the last juicy worm of summer. The only thing that saved me from demise was her light-haired husband, in dark trousers, standing behind her red top.

The responsibility of inflicting revenge melted away with the same ease as the real, fanny-grabbing perpetrator. It finally registered in my fuddled brain that along with grabbing the wrong man, I had also grabbed... the wrong side of the man.

Not able to contain his glee the object of my assault stood guard between his wife and me. Her loud and unrelenting tirade of verbal abuse brought my friend along with store security.

I sat in shock, sprawled on the store floor. My Comrade in this Granny Caper helped me up as we tried to explain that we were not perverted grandmothers gone astray but both victims of a fanny grabbing man roaming the store and we were just trying to catch him.

Minutes later we were all standing around the cluttered desk of the security guard while, The Wife informed the guard she wanted to press charges. The Husband refused and tried to calm his smoldering spouse. My senior age does not seem to have any effect on his smiling face, which only added fuel to the blaze of his wife's anger.

My friend shoved her elbow in my side and tried to hide a grin when she sees the young husband wink at me from behind his wife's back. My thoughts were, "Oh Brother! He thinks he has made my day because I am a granny." My friend whispers in my ear, "It's probably the only time he has truly enjoyed shopping with his wife."

The eyes of the brown, wrinkled-faced security guard twinkled but his resigned grunt spoke volumes. At the end of the interrogation, we were given a warning and the strongest of suggestions to do our shopping elsewhere from now on. The irate wife left with a jubilant husband in toll. You could tell this was to be a shopping story he would be sharing with friends for many days to come.

My best friend and I discussed our shopping adventure in the car on our way home. Her roar of laughter is contagious, and the instant replay of our shopping event bubbles up and transformed our mood. We again became those two young girls from our past, with a need for adventure and a sense of renewed women's equality.

We realized that we are still card-carrying members of the sisterhood and today were elevated to Super Seasoned Granny status. Our new pledge was to be strong of heart and courageous in spirit, protect children and challenge all the wrongdoers that have the misfortune to come our way.

A Remarkable Thing Happened

By Linda J Shook

The corn has been picked and squirrels scurry with nuts.
The Old North Wind blows us about and starts to cut.

A remarkable thing happened that brightens the day,
Christmas showed signs of coming and joy gave way.

Christmas music and holiday smells all mingle together,
Snow covers the scenery, and we smile about the weather.

Fleece coats, warm woolen mittens help us enjoy the snow.
Caroler's singing and lighted trees create a merry glow.

Red bows and red noses all become part of our jolly scene,
bright presents, and decorated cookies fill children's dreams.

Slowly but surely... peace seeps back into our life,
We remember again, the bliss of not having strife.

Our spirit fills with cheer, we hold tight to that which is holy.
Jesus' day of birth changes our hearts... and we sing his glory.

God reminds us again... what Jesus' life is all about,
teaching love to this world to remove our doubt.

Celebrate this Holy Season and keep it dear,
let it be a time when blessings draw near.

Beloved, I pray God lift your heart and fill it with his light,
lessen your heavy yoke of living, so it doesn't fit so tight.

May this year's ringing of the Christmas bells,
find you and family happy and well.

A Special Brand of "Fishin"

By L. J. Shook

This story is about my father, the fisherman. He wasn't the hip boots, fancy fly-casting type that you see in the movies. He was of more an everyday, garden-variety type of fisherman. He owed a couple good poles, a stringer, tackle box and of course, a good knife.

It wasn't until I became an adult with children of my own that I realized that dad didn't just go "fishin," for fish he liked to spin a tale and play practical jokes also. Dad would throw out his tale and most of the time you didn't know you had been hooked until you heard his rumble of laughter.

My father, brother and son are all owners of the wonky gene from dad's gene pool. I would watch them coming from the garage to the house walking in form like ducks in a row. First dad, then my brother, and last my son. They were lined up in an unconscious order of seniority and experience. It wasn't so much that they looked alike but more their mannerisms and a peculiar kind of humor that bonded them together and set them apart from the rest of the world.

I'm sure the reason is some mutated gene passed down from my father's side of the family. The curse of being first-born lay heavily on my shoulders and my dose of mutated gene was more concentrated. My saving Grace is this gene doesn't respond as well to the female gender. You had to be a male to fully glean the effects of this peculiar part of our DNA. Passing the gene to my son has made him and my father almost clone-like in their behavior and best buddies from the time my son could walk and follow along behind his papaw.

A long winter had the male trio restless and longing for summer. Some time during a prolonged cold snap the plans for a summer fishing trip were hatched, my son was especially excited. This was to be a weekend trip and far enough away to spend the night. You can't call it a camping trip if you don't camp, they told the rest of us.

When my son was small, he used to spend the night with my parents and sleep in his papaw's T-shirts. His own PJs were never good enough. Of course, he would always get scared and climb into the middle of my parents' king-size bed with dad on one side and mom on the other. I think it was caused by all those, "bears in the basement stories," that dad told with dramatic sound effects. My dad knew from experience that my son would wiggle until he was crosswise in the bed so he could put his feet on one person, and feel the face of the other person, to make sure someone was close by for protection. Every time you experienced a hand on your face you would be startled awake. After a few years of a scared son crawling into your bed when he heard a noise that scared him you came to expect it as part of the territory of being a parent or grandparent to this particular child.

The whole family drew a sigh of relief when my son became old enough to fight the night monster by himself. By this time my brother was married with children of his own and had never learned the sleeping habits of my Son.

Summer finally arrived along with the long-awaited fishing trip. The full day of fishing tired out the trio, so they cleaned their day's catch and settled down for a nice dinner of cooked fish over an open fire. During dinner the sleeping arrangements were hatched. Dad innocently and with a self-sacrificing attitude, volunteered to sleep in the cab of the truck leaving the truck bed with camper shell for my son and brother. Both volunteered to sleep in the cab so dad could sleep in the back where there was more room, but dad insisted. The trio, tired from their long day, fell asleep quickly.

Suddenly my brother was startled awake because a hand

had felt his face, he sat up quickly and banged his head on the camper shell. With heart pounding he was ready for battle. But no one was around except my son sleeping quietly on the other side of the truck. Finally, he calmed himself down and drifted back to sleep and then he felt a hand on his face again. This time he saw the hand attached to the arm of his sleeping nephew. With great irritation my brother moved to the farthest corner of the truck and settled down, but "The Hand," woke him up again. My son had rolled over in his sleep to get warm and was close enough to feel my brother's face for the third time.

My brother collects his blankets and pillow, left the truck, and stomps out to the picnic table in a major huff. He is too big to lie on the table, so he makes do next to the table and lies down. Soon he realizes he is sleeping in ant heaven, and he is covered in ants. A wild dance rids him of most of his tiny friends.

Knowing my brother, he is now ready to stomp the ground with all the fury of a mad bull. As the story goes, he fumbles around in the dark tripping over roots in search of a rock-free, ant-free plot of ground. He just wants sleep... anywhere that is free from the hand in the back of the truck.

My brother stumbles over some mossy grass and decides to roll up in his sleeping bag and quickly falls into an exhausted sleep. The morning sun is starting to light the eastern sky, when my brother again feels a hand on his face, he is too tired to do anything but open one bleary eye to see his nephew lying beside him on the ground asleep. I am certain that my brother didn't know that my son also walks in his sleep (but my dad did). All the grandparents knew from experience of my son's sleeping habits.

My brother's grizzly bear roar of frustration wakes everyone within earshot of their campsite.

The women in the family were all surprised when the old, blue, Chevy pickup, pulls into the driveway a few hours early. We knew something was up when Dad got out of the truck grinning. My brother was dragging behind with red-rimmed eyes and whiskered face.

It took all the time, during the drive home, for my brother's sleep-deprived brain to figure out that dad had set him up. As he entered the house, he points his finger at dad and said, ***"You did it on purpose, didn't you!!!"*** My father could no longer contain his laughter, and his grin turned into a belly laugh. Dad knew that my son would feel my brother's face but my brother leaving the truck and my son following him was just a bonus for dad that he thoroughly relished.

The whole family enjoyed the fun as the story unfolded. My brother was as mad as an old wet hen since the joke was on him. He took his gear and went home in a huff where he could finally sleep... with no interruptions.

Like pawns on a checkerboard, dad had been practicing his own special brand of fishing... again.

A Survival Guide for Grandma

By L. J. Shook

I have concluded; my father's side of the family has a wonky gene passed down for generations. This trait rarely affects the females but always the males. It turns them into some kind of Tom Sawyer-Huck Finn hybrid with rascal tendencies.

My father, brother, son and all my grandsons are in full possession of this gene. So, you can imagine my dismay when my daughter asked me to watch her two boys for the summer. My grandsons were eight and twelve years old at the time, one had attention deficit disorder (ADD) and the other attention deficit/hyperactivity disorder (ADHD). Any one of three conditions; being eight and twelve-year-old boys, ADD and ADHD, or the wonky gene pool could turn a grandmother's hair white but having all three together takes survival skills of the fittest. Here is the strategy I used to survive my grandchildren.

1. *Never fall asleep, close your eyes, or put yourself in a prone position, even if you are sick.*
   Your headache will become a nightmare if you lie down and appear vulnerable. You will be putting yourself in danger of pranks, being tied up or having lipstick on your forehead.

2. *Never, never, turn your back on them.*
   Learn to be a wall hugger. I should have known there was a plot being hatched when sudden silence permeated the room. Being still was never part of their nature so quiet periods signaled danger...danger. Foam bullets suddenly flew by my head, their cat attacked my leg, and I was mooned by two bare bottoms as I turned to see what they could possibly be up to now.

3. *Embrace free child labor.*

When the momentum of unruly behavior has taken hold, making them do cleaning chores seemed to take the steam out of their antics. Having them fold laundry, especially their mother's underwear, would strike terror into their little pea brains.

4. *Never be afraid to modify superpowers.*

Boys at this age devour comic books, superhero movies, and pretend to have superpowers. My eight-year-old grandson informed me the only superpower he had was being able to pass gas so terrible that people ran from the room. He never figured out that slipping probiotics with his vitamins was kryptonite this grandma used on her talented superhero.

5. *Never bat an eye, twitch, or let them see you sweat.*

Practice a stern face and a mean glare in the mirror before leaving home. If you want to smile or laugh at their antics, then leave the room until the urge passes. You will have plenty of time to laugh and tell their stories of mischief later. Remember you are outnumbered, old and cannot show weakness.

6. *Always practice what you preach.*

Do not expect behavior from your grandchildren you are not willing to practice yourself. This was my biggest challenge. One intense, battle-weary, morning I decided to give the boys some air and preempt their usual mayhem. I wanted to help my daughter by taking items to Goodwill. After physically dealing with the fight over who sat where in the car or the eight-year-old's crying episode because he had to relinquish his out-grown clothes and old sleeping bag, my stress level was maxed out before leaving my daughter's driveway. As I started to pull away from the donation door at Goodwill an old man drove into the exit lane blocking my way. Instead of pulling forward so I could leave or giving me space so I could pull out, he rudely motioned for me to back up. I could have done that but suddenly there were red spots in front of my eyes, and I smelled smoke... It was coming from my ears. I put the car in neutral and crossed my arms. He continued his air jabs for me to back up, but I had already fallen over the edge, and I was determined "I would die first." *I was way beyond my limit of dealing with males behaving badly.* The old coot stepped from his car as if coming towards me but after seeing my face, he turned to go tattle to the store attendant, leaving me blocked in. My first instinct was to jump from the car, wrestle him to the ground and punch him in the eye. I knew I could take him; he was an old man using a cane. Then *my own words came back to me,* those same words that I had preached to the boys all summer, "There is too much violence in the world. Why does the first solution to everything have to be violence?" I took a deep breath.

7. *Teach your grandchildren not to be bullied.*
    At the Goodwill Store I took a deep breath and did the only thing I would consider in my state of deranged thinking. I pulled forward into the slight opening afforded me and inched my car relentlessly backward and forward multiple times, barely missing the support column of the drive-thru and the old man's car, until I could squeeze my way from the building and exit, WITHOUT BACKING UP, as the old geezer and attendant stood gaping with open mouths. I wasn't sure who I was more upset with, the old fool or myself. My foot became possessed from my built-up frustration and floored the gas pedal. The back of my car fishtailed as I hard-shifted the gears. The boys, who had remained dead silent, suddenly burst forth, "Faster, Grammy, faster!" The twelve-year-old yells, "Grammy I didn't know you could drive so fast." The eight-year-old threw his arms up and cheered from the backseat. "It's okay Granny I gave him the finger for you." I

was driving too recklessly to reprimand him. Finally at the end of my day, I was used up and exhausted as I wearily dragged myself home, but could honestly say that I did, with white knuckle restraint, practice what I preached, and showed the boys that bullies are everywhere, and violence is not the only solution to a problem.

8. *Choose your battles.*
   The best battle plan is chosen from a warm heart rather than a hot head. It is better to teach your grandchildren a hundred ways to solve a problem than teach them there is only one way.

9. *Never teach your grandchild blind obedience.*
   Males buy into the blind obedient idea. Fathers want blind obedience from their children because it is easier to parent and keep control. If you teach unquestioned, blind obedience, without earned trust or good parenting then your grandchildren will always need someone to think for them to feel secure. Do you really want drug dealers, sex perverts, and extreme terrorist groups to have control over your children because you have pre-programmed them for blind obedience? It is better that a child independently makes the right choice than to always be forced into one. If I teach my grandchildren self-respect and good values they can determine their own future, not me... and not someone else.

10. *Talk to your grandchildren about life and making mistakes.*
    When my grandkids make a mistake, I ask them how they can make a better decision next time. I told them about one of my mistakes. At six I decided to drive my parents' jeep. I watched and planned it out for days. I waited till mom was hanging clothes on the line, then I grabbed her keys, and slipped into the jeep, turned the key, pushed in the clutch, and shifted the gear, just like I had watched her do. By looking

through the steering wheel and standing on the floorboard, I made it a half mile down the road before the jeep stalled and rolled into the ditch. I told my grandsons how lucky I was, not to have been hurt, except for the spanking my mother gave me. I explained that I could have hurt other people or wrecked the only transportation that my parents had. I never expect perfection from the boys but improving bad behavior is essential. It is okay if you screw up but make better choices next time and most importantly learn from your mistakes.

11. *Teach your grandkids how to have dreams.*
I talked with the boys about their dreams so they will feel real and attainable. No one is born believing they want to be a criminal; it is usually taught behavior or comes from desperation. The difference between an athlete and a criminal is a person who is encouraged to believe that dreams are possible. Too many times children are told they are inadequate and pressured to be mediocre. The greatest sin of family dysfunction is that, as a child, you are exposed to poverty of spirit and convinced you cannot achieve anything bigger than your family's circumstances.

12. *Be brave enough and loving enough to rein in your grandchildren when needed.*
Politeness, consideration, and manners do not need to be outdated. I explained to my grandsons how love should act and how abuse, prejudice and control are never love. I think that if a child is taught love and is shown forgiveness, they will understand how love works. Love and hate are both taught behaviors, so teach your grandchildren well. Not all children in this world are taught acceptance or know love and it is showing up in our society, our schools, and our world.

13. *I saved the best for last... use affection and grace every day.*
Overzealous discipline and harsh words can leave fingerprints with permanent scars. The real purpose for a punishment is to get their attention and let them know what they did was serious enough you want it to stop, <u>now</u>; taking away their self-worth by calling names or using out-of-perspective punishment that doesn't match the crime should never be part of the process. Even though my grandsons need high-alert parenting, they are <u>always</u> worth it. If I show the boys love and grace now, then hopefully they will use it with me in the future when I am nutty as a fruit cake and forgetting everything.

I told my daughter that my sanity was at risk after my summer with the boys especially after they pulled the fire alarm at the library, after they surprised attacked me and tried to tie me to a chair, after they poured shampoo on the cat, after they commando rigged packets of catsup under the toilet seat, after they threw the neighbor boy's shoes on the roof, and after dealing with the whole situation when they tried to flush an apple down the toilet. The boy's mother... my daughter, informs me that it was okay and not to worry because I have not been right for years and still suffer from the effects that she, her brother and sister put me through when they were growing up.

Here I am a few years later and only now just beginning to feel a little peace in thinking that I can survive my grandchildren, when God injects his sense of humor into my life. Last week I had a battle and a major power struggle with one of my grandchildren because I would not let one of them drive the car. This did not come from my oldest grandson who is now seventeen years old, but from his four-year-old little sister, who was dead serious about thinking she should drive.

My four-year-old granddaughter was becoming way too bossy. She is cute and the youngest in the family and relentlessly tells her four teenage brothers what to do and the boys would carry her around and do whatever she says because she is cute and the baby. I have concerns that this bossy behavior will develop into a permanent pattern. It was time for Grandma to modify miss cutie pants thinking.

While babysitting I talked with Rylee about her becoming too bossy. I suggested it would be fun to play a new game called role play and I would act and say all the things she would say, and she was to pretend to be me and say all the things she thought I would say. I felt Rylee was starting to understand how bossy she had become from the answers I gave when acting like her, the role playing was fun, we laughed, and it was working great until the end of the day when it was time to pick up her mother from work.

Since my granddaughter was role playing me, she climbs under the steering wheel and insists on driving the car. When I told her you don't have a driver's license, and you are only four, she had a major full-blown meltdown like only a four-year-old can have. Who would have thought that relinquishing the role of playing grandma could be so eventful?

God just bombed me with a little blond-haired reminder that he has a long memory involving me driving my parent's car at six and showed me God's wonderful sense of humor.

I am starting to get a sick feeling that my granddaughter might be the first female in the family to inherit my father's wonky gene...God help us all.

A Whopping Fish Tale

By L. J. Shook

I guess you can find humor almost anywhere, if you're willing to give a little time to look and listen. I know for me; funny things and humorous stories just seem to sneak up on me when I least expect them. This is what happened to me the other day, in the middle of work stress, dealing with high maintenance personalities, and unreasonable work duties, a funny story came along and bumped into me and made me pay attention.

This funny story came bundled up in the disguise of a grandpa. He was tall and young looking for his years, with dark hair, handsome features and he didn't have a tooth in his mouth. He started his story by talking about the troubles he was having trying to keep all his women happy. That got my attention right away. I started watching him, not so he would notice, and wondered just how many women problems could a toothless grandpa have?

As he talked, I began to understand that the females he was talking about, was a wife of many years, and a little granddaughter who loved him unconditionally because he was grandpa and didn't need teeth.

Grandpa's pride in his little granddaughter was evident by the twinkle in his eyes and the love in his voice when talking about his favorite little girl. His story began when he bought his favorite little girl a pink Barbie Doll, fishing pole. He had attached a rubber worm to the plastic hook, with the promise of taking her fishing real soon.

I guess grandpa just didn't understand what, "real soon." meant to the pint-size female in his life. While grandpa was cooking dinner, he heard a loud squeal from the other room and his little granddaughter was calling to him, "Paw... Paw, I caught one, I caught one."

Grandpa ran into the room just in time to see one of his prize aquarium fish, worth hundreds of dollars, being reeled in by his little granddaughter. I imagine when you're a fish who has lived in an aquarium for years, even a rubber worm looks good. Grandpa managed to save his favorite fish while pulling his granddaughter off the top of his 150-gallon aquarium.

I not sure this grandpa will ever figure out how to keep all his women happy, but he has a new appreciation for the determination of his favorite little girl and one whopper of a funny fish story to tell about the fish that really did get away.

Answered Prayer

By L. J. Shook

Her prayer was small, young, and intense, like she was. Susan was seven years old when her young prayers started, but she had the hard life experiences of someone much older. The way of her birth, as Susan told the story, seemed to reflect a pattern that her life would follow for the rest of her years.

Susan is a special friend of mine, part of a group of women aged twenty to sixty. Three of us worked at the same newspaper, the fourth and youngest of the group is a cousin of Susan's.

It started as a girl's night out after visiting the neighborhood pizza restaurant and continued into the wee hours of morning when we drifted back to my apartment. The screened porch let in the warm night air and flickered the candles that we lit to diminish the darkness.

We did what females have always done...share our special moments and stories. Susan's story was the last to be told and the haunting honesty of her story took my breath. When Susan talked, she was unaware of the way her words impacted the women in our group.

Susan's story started on the day of her birth. Her mother was resting on the couch and was awakened by a hard contraction, a few contractions later Susan entered this world and lay crying on the couch at the feet of her mother. I remember thinking it was hard to tell who had put more effort into the birth, the mother, or the newborn baby.

Susan was the tenth child, born to Irish parents. Her father was a hardworking, hard drinking man that went to work every day at the Post Office to provide for his large Catholic Clan. Her mother was a stay-at-home mom. The nightly ritual of her mother's drinking came after putting all the children, still living at home, to bed. The six pack of beer always required a bathroom visit and Susan's mother had to pass the bedroom that Susan shared with her sisters.

The familiar sound of footsteps signaled Susan to start her prayer. As her mother's uneven steps became louder Susan did her nightly ritual of throwing the blanket from her bed to the floor. Then she would begin her intense prayer, and it was always the same: "Please God, just once, just one time let my mother check on me to see if I am cold and need to be covered up. Please, Father in heaven, just one time."

Reality is a hard taskmaster and whether from too many children or too many nights of beer, her mother never once exercised that age-old maternal instinct on her youngest and tenth child. This simple act is a motherly instinct unless those instincts have been drowned out, by something more important than your child.

We all struggle for the understanding of why the denial of love can have such a strong and long-lasting hold. Susan has lived thirty plus years with the pain of never hearing the words, "I love you," from her parents and still wondering why God did not answer children's prayers.

The women in our group, mothers of all ages, wiped tears from our eyes. The heaviness in our hearts felt like a group pain for all the children, like Susan, who have grown up feeling unloved and never cherished.

Three decades have a way of wearing down sharp edges, and the mother who spent so many years attached to a bottle of alcohol to disconnect from her life, now needs a bottle of oxygen to have life.

As much as life changes, so much of it remains the same. Susan's father passed away last year and now Susan is the only sibling, out of ten kids, who takes the time from her busy life to care for her sick parent. These acts of nursing are performed out of duty but not love. Those seeds of neglected love, planted all those years earlier, did in fact take root, grow, and now bare their own fruit.

While her sick mother naps Susan rests her weary head in a chair near the hospital bed, listening to the sounds of her mother's labored breathing. Susan's eyes grew heavy. Too many hours of being deprived of sleep, trying to manage a full-time job, teenage son, and sick parent, have taken their toll. A movement is heard in the room, Susan listens but is too weary to open her eyes so she waits.

A blanket, pulled from her sick mother's bed, gently covers Susan's body as it is placed over her by her dying mother's hand. Susan's heart flutters and she is reminded of her childhood prayer. Tears escaped from the corner of her closed eyes.
God never forgot that innocent child's prayer, even if that prayer had to be worked on for thirty years.

By L. J. Shook

My life was comfortable living in an apartment designed for retired and fixed income people. Even though it was not my dream place to live, it was safe, clean, and affordable. As amazing as life is it has a way of throwing you curve balls.

The original owner of my building never put expensive maintenance into the facility and when the costly repairs could no longer be ignored, he sold the complex. The new owners wanted to push out the older people with limited incomes so they could rent to young, upward-moving, professionals but the government contract had the conditions of our rent locked to certain guidelines.

The new owners started by increasing our rent as high as the guidelines would allow, then they added new charges for our parking spaces and moved the parking lot half of a block down the street so the people with bad hearts and bad knees and other health issues found it hard to walk to the parking lot.

Next, they charged adsorbent fees to do laundry and even added dumpster costs for our trash. Each new fee was targeted to slowly increase the total costs of living in the building beyond the fixed incomes of the senior renters. This had the effect they wanted and effectively squeezed out the old people without getting the owners in trouble with the government program. They obviously had done this before.

My independent spirit rebelled but realized that it would be impossible for me to fight corporate America by myself. The questionable victory of living in a place I didn't really like wasn't worth the time, battle and cost it would take. The time was right for me to find a place where I really wanted to live.

Regardless of where I looked the rent was always out of my

reach. Time was running out for my exit and if I didn't leave soon, I would be forced to sign a lease for another year.

After much prayer I was guided to a place in a small town about ten miles away. The rent was still higher than I wanted, and my limited income caused me to have a very tight budget for the other bills and necessities needed to live. But this was the place God had guided me to in my hour of need. I took a leap of faith and moved with the belief that God would show me a way to manage this new life-altering change.

Each month I managed to get by and with the passage of time I became more secure that all was going to work out for me. An old friend was sure I would fail. She told me constantly that I wouldn't make it. She told all her family and our friends how I would soon be homeless. It was like Henny Penny, running around my life squawking my demise about the sky falling.

I tried to ignore her but still felt the effects of all the negative energy she was pumping into the air around me and wondered about the reason behind her thinking that I would fail. I prayed for God's help in showing me how to make my life work and... to just plain shut my friend up.

One evening my friend picked me up for a planned event. It was dark when she let me out in my driveway, and I watched for her to leave before turning out the porch light. She sat in my driveway for a long time, and I wondered why it was taking her so long to leave and started to worry about her having a health issue. Just when I put my hand on the doorknob to go outside and check on her, she backed out of the driveway.

After a couple months she finally told me about the angel dressed like a man who stepped out of the shadows by my porch and told her to, "Back off and leave me alone, and to immediately stop telling me and everyone she met that I was going to fail," then he instantly disappeared. She knew it was an angel because of the way he had appeared and disappeared and the way he made her feel.

It took my friend a long time to tell me about the Angel. He had scared her and made her feel ashamed with his blunt instructions, but she did as the Angel had instructed her to do.

I am surprised and forever grateful for my blessed protector watching over my life... in so many different and amazing ways.

Because I Can

By L. J. Shook

My childhood was filled with my father's love and blanket of protection, but that seemed like a long time ago. I hadn't felt protected since I was 19 years old and left my parent's home to become a bride. These are probably called the first pangs of growing up.

The age of women being protected seems to have long passed. You see it in old movies and some TV shows, and I think it is still part of a male's DNA but once a female has discovered she can handle most things herself the need for protection lessen.

When you think about the progress women have made in the last hundred years you realize that men had to give up some ground for women to be more equal. A hard lesson learned is that men aren't going to give up their turf willingly. Men don't and can't give way easily. Watch basketball, football, or any competitive sport and it will prove this fact. The male logic and personality are not made to give way easily. I'm not saying this is good or bad, it is just the way things are.

My teenage son taught me one of my first experiences of how men are still guarding their turf. My divorce was a scary period in all our lives, but my thirteen-year-old son's reaction was more seriously acted out than his two sisters. It felt like my son's main and only goal in life was to make me and his sisters as miserable as possible, with a lot of success I might add. At my most frustrated point I asked him, "Why are you acting like this?" His answer is something that I'll always remember and have referred to frequently. He stood with a defiant stance, that only a teenage boy can achieve, and with a look that was not quite child, not adult but most certainly all male, he said, "BECAUSE I CAN!" That answer rocked my reality. How did a thirteen-year-old come to think he was so entitled to act in any horrible way he felt like towards females, his sisters and me and think he could get by with it and it was okay for him to do so?

It made sense to me that when dealing with my son and later with other males who tried to use the, "Because I can," attitude regarding females; that it was time for this behavior to be lost forever.

I remember when one of our presidents was going through a sex scandal, he was asked under oath why he lied and his answer was the same as my son's, he said, "Because I Can." This caused me to realize this was no small-town condition but stemmed from an attitude of entitlement that most men seem to have and use to deal with women too much of the time.

In no way am I saying that all men act like this. Men don't use this behavior all the time, but most men use it some of the time. I have even experienced my three-year-old grandson using this behavior on rare occasions.

I don't know a woman alive that hasn't experienced this attitude from a male. When I asked other females whether they had encountered this behavior all of them, 100%, answered with a resounding yes, regardless of their age or economic status. Even men will admit they have experienced this kind of entitled attitude used on them by other males.

It took several years to refine and be comfortable using this information. Not that I didn't use "No you can't" often, but it took a while before it became second nature for me. Now I use it unconsciously. After so many years of being single I am still amazed at how well those three little words, "No you can't," work on men... all men. For the men that do have and practice this bad behavior it has becomes a habit or an excuse to use when they are angry, frustrated, or feeling vulnerable in their life.

When working at a Radio Station it was my first big chance to be a copywriter. An older, self-made man, whose family came from Romania, as a child, owned the station. The owner was coarse, abrasive and verbally abusive to his family, his staff and clients. His policy was to hire single women with dependent children who were needy enough and desperate enough to continue working regardless of his abuse. I overheard him telling his policy to a newly hired male employee. After several teary journeys home at the end of the day I decided to start applying my, "No you can't," theory to his highly offensive behavior. Even though my job was something I needed for my survival and my dream chance to write professionally, and the thing that I had worked towards for a long time was being put at risk, nothing was worth returning to another abusive condition in my life.

The daily practice of the owner was to call the station from home and whoever answered the phone, usually the Office Manager/Copywriter, which was me, was put through a rigorous session of degrading, condescending attitudes and general verbal abuse. The way I dealt with him was to act busy and put him on hold and not come back to answer his phone line again or reroute him to the one, "Barbie-Doll," blond in our office that he didn't abuse. When she wasn't available then I disconnected my boss or accidentally on purpose hung up on him. It took two weeks before my behavior sunk into his thick head, but he finally got the message. One day he cornered me in the front office and demanded to know, in front of the entire staff, why I wouldn't talk to him on the phone. This is an old and affective form of intimidation used by older men.

With a steady stare I told him, "When you are ready to be courteous, treat me with respect and act more professionally than I will be more than willing to take your phone calls." the whole office grasps at the same time, and it vibrated around the room as one audible sound. With a sly smile on his face his voice boomed, "I could fire you." I firmly returned his smile and said, "I could get paid more at a fast-food restaurant." Being a coward was never one of my faults, hundreds of other faults, but not being a coward. So, I continued to smile and make eye contact and quietly asked him a question. "Why do you do it?" I thought I knew the reason for his behavior but didn't think he would be honest enough to admit it, but he replied, "Because I can," those same exact words that my son had used.

He didn't fire me and from that day on grudgingly treated me with the respect that I had stood my ground for. The owner still treated the other girls with his abusive behavior but over the next few weeks a strange thing started happening. His phone calls were getting disconnected more and more as the other girls started taking a stand. No one got fired and the owner grudgingly gave up his old turf of intimidation and verbal abuse because there was no longer fertile ground to sow his seeds of bad behavior. Men will only give you what you expect from them, rarely willing and almost always it must be upon demand.

A good friend and I were discussing bosses over coffee one morning and she told me about her boss. She had worked for a prominent eye surgeon for eight years, but he had progressively got more stressed after his marriage and children came along, and this caused him to become verbally and even physically abusive. He would berate his staff in front of the patients and had even resorted to throwing instruments at them on occasion. My friend had finally reached a point when she was no longer willing to tolerate this kind of daily behavior, so she started looking for another job. Her boss was the best eye surgeon in Cincinnati, and she would have to take a cut in pay if she took another job. The salary cut would be a financial hardship but sometimes happiness comes at a price, and she was willing to make the change.

The doctor found out about her job hunting when calls for references started coming into the office. The doctor called my friend into his office. With genuine hurt feelings he wanted to know why, after eight years, she wanted to leave. My friend told the doctor that his behavior had gotten worse over the years and even though she loved her job, working for him wasn't worth the amount of stress and abuse he displayed daily.

The truth and honesty of her words upset the doctor and with true remorse he told her he was sorry. He promised to work on correcting his behavior if she stayed. As she was leaving his office she turned back and asked him a question. "Why have you been acting like this?" his answer was, "Well, I guess it's because I can."

Amazing, those words, those same words all expressed by the male gender, from the young to the old, from the businessman to the professional, separated by time and space but still using the same behavior and the same words.

If you look back in history, then you will see that men had the whole burden of support for the family but that also meant they had total control over finances and decision making. When women went to work during World War I & II to build airplanes and machinery needed for the war, they also had to run the home and keep the family going while the men were gone. After this level of independence, they were no longer willing to turn over their hard-earned money and the right to decide their future to men again. This was a huge problem for men coming home from World War I & II because they were used to having total control over home and hearth and didn't want to let go of this old pattern of control, but the women through this shift in society, were no longer programmed to be submissive.

I worked with a thirty-year-old black woman in health care, and she told me a story about her parents. Her father had abused her mother physically and emotionally her entire life while she was growing up. Her parents were getting old now with health issues, but her father would still occasionally slap her mother around. One day her mother finally reached her breaking point. She went into the bedroom and got her husband's gun and sat down at the table where he was drinking coffee, she laid the gun on the table and with quiet determination told her husband, "If you ever hit me or abuse me again, I will shoot your sorry ass."

The woman I worked with told me her father never once hit or abused her mother again from that point on.

In all the years that I have been telling men, "No you can't," I have never once been fired and rarely yelled at. Males usually give me a boyish grin, like a child being caught with their hand in the cookie jar. I think some of the old programming is still in the genes but when losing control, men do not want to give way easily, especially on letting go of power. Just look at the election this year if you have any doubts.

It is important that we all become the best version of the person that we are meant to be without all the games and past issues coloring our future.

Have courage and be honest with yourself and the people around you, and never be afraid to say, "No you can't, to any and all of the males or any person who tries to use bad or degrading behavior and words on you."

The world needs your courage, and it will become a better place because you are brave enough to stand up for it.

Bent Lips

It started out slowly and barely touched the middle.
It wiggled and squirmed before it could settle.
My face distorted and then started to convey,
crinkling the corners, as my mouth gave way.

What is this strange phenomenon that just occurred?
It changed my mood, causing old thoughts to blur.
It was crazy and sane, all mixed up into one.
Whatever it is... becomes transforming and fun.

The birth of a smile was what started the sparkle.
And caused me to stop and I began to marvel.
How could such a small act brighten my way,
chase away stress and all that is frayed?

I was reminded once again what a smile could do,
It opens a heart and gives birth to ideas anew.
What a gift and a treasure... I want to share,
All the smile-sunbeams I can possibly spare,

Giving to strangers and all that seem weary,
helping to spread light in all the dreary.
So, if you find a moment with nothing to do,
share a smile and brighten one another's blues.

By L. J. Shook

Bertha

By L J Shook

Now that I am retired my life is freer and there is more time for hobbies, crafts, along with writing and painting classes and a whole bunch of new and delightful things that I rarely had time for during my busy younger years.

One of the things that happens is that retired people start to question themselves and wonder how much good they really did during their life. Did they find their purpose for coming to earth and fulfill it?

When I see my adult children and grandchildren behaving in a way, I consider to be dysfunctional, and see them struggle with relationships, jobs, and life, then I question myself on whether it is something I caused by my parenting

During the last several conversations I have had with my retired friends we have all had similar thoughts. Our children are in a whole different place now and the values that applied to us when growing up, and we tried to teach our children no longer have a place to function in society these days. So along with the world being different comes the feeling that as an older person the things we say, or think are not considered valuable and at best only tolerated.

Instead of wallowing in the mirky waters of old age and self-doubt I decided to look back and try to remember the good I have done in my life. I was profoundly surprised there was so much to think about. Many prayers for people I knew and didn't know but saw a problem or burden where help was needed, and a silent prayer was sent. I have helped change lives a few times and I know I saved a couple of lives when working on the crisis line.

Working as a caregiver for my parents and later with Hospice and health care agencies, being a Reiki Master, or as a counselor for group homes for the mental and physical handicap has blessed my life with hundreds of opportunities to give love and support when I saw a need. My life stories surrounded me like a warm blanket and the realization of the good I have done far outweighed the mistakes and errors I have made during my life.

While looking back, there was one memory that caused me to stop, ponder and smile, her name was Bertha. It was during a time when I worked as a copywriter for a Radio station in a small town. Bertha was a woman in her late sixties who came into the station occasionally to sell small greeting ads. The little bit of money she received helped supplement her income, which was needed because she took care of a sick husband and a special needs son still at home. Bertha was small, cheerful with twinkling eyes and grey hair and you would never know her plight in life unless you had conversations with her. Since in society's eyes she was considered, an old woman, rarely did the younger people bother to talk to her or asked her about her life.

The manager of the radio station was the son of the owner who had retired, and I think Bertha was a left-over employee from his father's time at the station and since Bertha did bring in revenue the son kept her on but basically ignored her.

Bertha had a sweet grandmother's way about her, and she could have sold buttons to a zipper maker. The manager didn't recognize Berth's talent, the ads she was selling were as worn as an old barn that had lost all its paint, but she was still able to sell them. The son had his own sales team that sold the big advertising ads, and he favored his top salesperson who looked like a Barbie Doll, so Bertha was almost invisible.

I talked to Bertha when time allowed and knew her ads were mostly geared for holidays and special occasions. She had been struggling with money lately because of medical expenses due to her husband's new health problems. The holidays were just around the corner, and it was a time when she could sell the most greeting ads. She was looking forward to the added money she could bring in, but she told me that the material was so old it was getting harder to sell.

I asked Bertha if I could write her some new ads. I found out what she wanted the ads to say and for what holidays and occasions she needed them. I was certain my boss wouldn't let me write the new ads at work and would consider them not important enough to take time away from the ads I wrote for his sales staff. I asked Bertha not to mention anything to him and I would write the ads on my own time. I told her if he didn't know maybe we could slip them in without his noticing. I had my suspicion he probably wasn't aware of what the old ads said anyway. So, I wrote Bertha pages and pages of new material that she could use for a long time.

One day I saw my boss come running from his office and head down the hall to Bertha's room. I had a sinking feeling I was in trouble but when he came back, he was smiling and never said a word to me.

My thoughts were right, and my boss didn't notice Bertha's new ads on his own, but she had taken those new ads and outsold his entire sales staff in terms of revenue, and that did get his attention. When Bertha was asked to explain how she had done it she was forced to tell him that I had written her new ads, but the rest was Bertha's skill. I don't know what else she said to him because he never said a word to me. I have a feeling the other side of the sweet grandma made a stand where I was concerned.

Bertha's extra money came when she needed it the most and the new ads would boost her income regularly for as long as she was able to work at her sales job. All Bertha needed was for someone to believe in her and give her a chance to help herself.

As for the worries about my parenting I am letting that go. If my children want to believe my parenting messed them up, then they can go get counseling... I am Retired.

Big City Beat

By L. J. Shook

The city roars down on me as I walk along the street. The noise vibrates off buildings and swishes around corners, pushing, pulling, chasing, me as I walk, trying to spin me in my tracks if I were not so heavily grounded, by baggage, natural and otherwise. Country-born and small town raised hasn't prepared me for this huge, constantly moving, breathing, throbbing place of sound, where towers of steel and brick, or ribbons of asphalt and concrete jostle for space with the busy beehive of people.

Riding the bus, a newfound experience, has brought me down to this human ant's perspective of city life. Curiosity gets the better of me and catches my reflection looking in storefronts, peering around corners, absorbing the rhythm of this alien place. Excitement and repulsion dance an Irish jig as each few steps discover new places to visit, to shop, to dine, and to browse.

The natives of this foreign space watch me from alleys, doorways, balconies, and office windows, some without my knowledge. They instinctively know that I am not from their land. There isn't that look of ease around me, nor do my actions reflect knowing where to go and how to get there in a hurry, that city dwellers know by nature. My face reflects questions, and in my eyes a look of uncertainty, expressing a lack of trust, in myself... in them. Their ways are foreign, and methods are not always to my liking or understanding. When looking into the faces of the city people I am greeted with hard and fast smiles. It seems everything in the city is done hard and fast, business, recreation, relationships and even sleeping. Then the next day starts all over again with living hard and moving fast to survive in this place called Cincinnati.

Buses zoom by and belch black diesel fumes with every stop

and start. News helicopters hover overhead in anticipation of traffic problems, crime, violence, even murder. The clunk and clang of misused cars rob what small measure of peace there is left when walking on the street. You can see vehicle-forced air move the brown edged leaves of trees polluted by acid rain, but no rustle is ever heard.

The everyday business of being in this high-energy, high-performance place creates a constant low-level of stress. How do city dwellers live in this place where your brain is required to be forever in a state of readiness to survive the hard and fast, at a moment's notice without taking a quiet break?

After my prolonged exposure to this living, breathing place, called the city, I can feel a measure of rage bubbling below the surface of my being because there is no break for peace. Like the warning of an inactive volcano that periodically rumbles to remind the world that with the right circumstances an eruption is possible. You see the rage bubbling in the faces of the city born and bred. The rage shows itself when a person gives a rude finger jester to a driver, a curt word is yelled at an inconsiderate person. The nasty retorts so freely and quickly dispensed over trivial acts of human behavior, opinions or viewpoints.

I feel sorrow for the inter-city dwellers whose big attitudes and shallow manners try to cover up an ever-present lack of respect and consideration for other people, their surroundings, and especially themselves. They don't understand that there can be life without rage, but it is all they have known. The rage has become their heritage, a cloak, their badge of honor, a reason to punish and their excuse to act out frustrations and violence.

I don't want to know about this deep feeling of rage. I can understand it from my own moving too fast, being pushed too hard and the unrelenting pressure of no peace or quiet. It does take its toll. Like the constant crying of a baby, the city literally can get on your nerves.

In a way the city reminds me of my childhood, when I would lay in tall grass face down with my chin on my arm and watch a parade of bugs and ants scurry from place to place. Some would carry objects twice their size, others had food, and some only a purpose, all in a hurry, survival depending on their swiftness. Now I am the ant in the tall jungle where speed is a necessary part of living, where the size of buildings diminishes humans to ants and workers to a hum in their concrete and steel beehives.

This city place, that cuts like a double-edged sword, one side severing your peace, and safety to the very bone; the reverse side cutting through the slow, sluggish everyday level of mediocrity, forcing you to function at a higher level of performance and understanding. The Big City holds you hostage and your heart captive at the same time. Who needs it and who can forget it?

I lived in the big city for a few years but eventually moved back to my hometown to leave the constant low-level stress behind. It took me a couple years to readjust to the slow talking, slow-moving small-town ideas and the forever limited mind sets. I'm glad that I had the experience of the big city but now I am equally glad that I am back where I can find peace and renew myself from all the everyday stress of living.

I now can enjoy the best of both worlds, visit the city for short periods of time to do business, shopping, and visit friends and then return to a place where I can renew and find peace. This life experience helped me find answers for the restlessness in me that I didn't know I had. It takes both the big city and quiet country to give me balance.

Thank God I have had the opportunity to experience the best of both.

Big Shift

By L. J. Shook

When you get older, past the half century mark, the intenseness of life seems to fall away. You are no longer interested in gladiator fights in the boardroom. The corporate ladder is replaced by the elevator because you have more important ways to spend your energy, and the true meaning of life is more of an issue than playing the game of life.

It is the time of downsize. The past age fifty people invented the condition of downsizing. Everyone thinks that it was some Yuppy that created this term, but our group has been doing it for years. It is brought about when our children leave home, and you suddenly have an empty nest. The big family house that you struggled for so many years to afford trying to impress the neighbors, is now too big to manage and too time- consuming to maintain.

All this new freedom from kids, home and high-end jobs opens more time to savor life instead of burning the candle at both ends, like we did when we were younger. I call this the Big Shift.

The Big Shift is wonderful. You see the past fifty group smiling but no one tells you why. They don't want you to know how great being fifty really is, otherwise everyone would be trying to get there. It is freedom from pressure cooker days of wondering whether you have raised your kids the right way. By the time you are fifty you will know if you have succeeded or screwed up. And to be perfectly honest, you have probably done a little of both. Whichever way you think it has gone your adult children will be more than willing and eager to give you their viewpoint on the subject.

If you take a good look at your children you will see that

sleepy pinched look you can only get when holding down a job and parenting younger kids. Our reward for all those years of suffering as a parent is grandchildren and they are the most glorious and wonderful gift of all.

My one misconception of the Big Shift was an illusion that there would be a parenting cut-off time, and the break would occur around the time the kids turned twenty or twenty-one. My grand thought was my job would be done and they could go the rest of the way by themselves.

Wrong, wrong, wrong, what a smoke screen!

Those dirty dogs from the generation before you kept this information from you like it was part of National Security. They learned the hard way that if you knew that parenting kids would go on forever then you might decide not to have any children, and they wouldn't get that glorious reward, of those grandkids. So, they kept tight-lipped and secretive about the "No cut-off time."

These days I no longer have day to day, minute by minute parenting duties like I had when the kids were younger instead I'm always on call, 24 hours a day 7 days a week. I have been pressed into more parenting since I hit fifty than I thought possible. I'm not talking about the, "I'm in your Business," type of parenting that gets all the laughs on TV. What I'm talking about is more of a running away and they are chasing after me type of parenting. That is one of the few drawbacks of being fifty plus, you can't run as fast as you used to.

My ex-mother-in-law was a lot like Raymond's mother on the TV show, "Everyone Loves Raymond," so I have always been extremely careful to not become "The Mother-In-Law." It's not that I don't see things that need to be changed or want to tell my children and their spouses about what I think they are doing wrong. I wouldn't be human if I didn't have those thoughts and feelings but when that urge happens I treat it like gas and go home and wait until it passes. To express my feeling would only create a big stink, (sorry about the pun), with nothing to show for it. I let my children come to me and then I know they are ready to hear my input and weigh what I say.

The wisdom that comes with the Big Shift is, it is impossible not to hear or remember something that has been said with anger or haste. It's not about what I think anyway, it's about how much I love my children and how I can best help them to make decisions for themselves, instead of them obeying my opinions or following my judgment. A truly loving parent is one who has given their children the tools they need to go out into the world and do their best.

You can't convince me that anyone in the Big Shift Group is truly enjoying a non-working son, hogging the TV and recliner while slurping down beer and food. Not to mention a daughter who breeds like a rabbit without a husband, filling those golden years with grandkids that never go home. Where is the Big Shift? You haven't shifted you have only extended. You need to *shift... shift!!!!!!*

The definition of grandkids is that they go home to a separate house. That is why they are wonderful and fun to be with because you aren't with them all the time. If you are with your grandkids all the time then you become an extended parent and are missing the wonders of being a "grand parent."

The Big Shift should also be a time to educate your kids that you were a **real person** before you became their parent and that you had a life that was edgy, young and daring. Let slip those stories that you have been hiding, about soaping windows on Halloween, Prom Night, and High School antics. Make those ripples in the pond now, while you are still convincing, before you start walking with a limp or doing the," one step at a time on the stairs routine," because of bad knees. Do it while there is still a little swing in the caboose and gas, (you can afford) in your tank.

The Big Shift is the time to create those stories your grandkids will be talking about when you are gone. My kids still laugh about my father, their grandfather, who convinced them there was a bear in the basement to try and scare them. Or the time he hid in the bushes blowing a train whistle at the neighbor as she rode by on her bicycle. They reminisce about the hundreds of times he played cards with them pretending to be losing only to have the winning hand. And they will never forget those endless fishing stories, camping trips and checker games.

My dad knew how to do the Big Shift the right way. He left his grandkids always laughing about the things he did. They never talk about how bad it was when he was dying of cancer, what they remember is the way he lived his life and how he impressed them with the strength of his personality and his great character.

Grab hold of that Big Shift period in your life and go strong while you are still fast enough to catch the grandbabies and get those sweet kisses. One day it will all be gone, like smoke in a summer breeze. This is your best time. Enjoy it while you are at your peak, seasoned, experienced and still have wind. Leave them all, kids and grandkids, shaking their heads, smiling and wondering what you will do next.

Always keep them wondering.

Bush Whacked

By L. J. Shook

Her toothless smile is what you first noticed when meeting Sue, but her heart was what you remembered. Sue was a neighborhood character that lived a few houses down from my parents. She gave color to the neighborhood with her abundant array of mixed-matched flowers, spilling over from the porch rail and steps leading up to her apartment. The flowers were as random and varied as her life had been. Like most neighborhoods in our small town, the experiences of her life spilled over into my parents' lives as well, especially my father's.

My dad was a fisherman in every sense of the word. Dad loved to do the normal kind of fishing where you used a pole, hook and bait but he also loved to go fishing for people. He could reel in a person just like a fish. He convinced his grandchildren there was a bear in his basement with vivid stories and disguised noises, even though they all knew better.

Dad would pretend he was losing at playing card and then surprise everyone with the winning hand. He would bait you, like a worm on a hook, with the idea that you could beat him at checkers by letting you jump one or two of his checkers so he could then in turn jump three or four of yours. One of my favorites was when he took my son fishing and had him thinking that to catch a fish you had to call, "Here fishy, fishy. Here fishy, fishy."

After dad's retirement my father had time on his hands and a lot more opportunity to figure out his mischief. On a visit to the Indiana State Fair, he bought a wooden whistle that sounded like a train. Dad used the whistle on the grandkids, neighborhood dogs, family members and then sat plotting just what he could do with his whistle next. Dad would rather play a joke than eat. There was no one safe from his jokes and that included his neighbor, Sue. Dad knew what time Sue went to work in the morning and when she came home in the evening.

One early morning, while the dew was still wet on the flowers, he slipped out the back door and hid in the bushes and laid in wait, so he would be in position when Sue mounted her bicycle to ride to work. He blew his train whistle just as she rode by.

The first time Sue was so startled that she ran her bicycle up on the sidewalk and into the neighbor's yard before she fell off. Of course, after that there was no stopping my father. Not regularly, but when she least expected it, he would hide in the bushes and blow his train whistle as she rode by. After a couple of times Sue figured out where the noise was coming from and that alone told her it had to be my father, who was notorious for playing his jokes. She never knew when Dad would strike with that train whistle and sometimes you could see her peddle her bike faster when she approached my parent's house.

Dad was faithful in his pursuit of surprising Sue with his bush-whack-tactics, and you could hear Sue's voice trailing behind her as she rode by, saying, "OH..... GIFFORD!!!" It became their running joke; she kidded him about his train whistle and hiding in the bushes he kidded her about being a reckless driver and falling off her bicycle.

The years piled up, one upon the other, and dad was still bush whacking Sue when she least expected. Then one summer the silence from the bushes became a stark reminder that dad was sick and no longer able to pull his joke on Sue when she rode by.

Dad's one wish was to die at home and Sue visited dad regularly, as he lay in his sick bed dying. Sue was as faithful in visiting him as he had been faithful in blowing his whistle at her. I think each in their own way showed how much it meant that someone cared enough to bother.

At my father's funeral a tearful Sue came up to me and said, "You know I never thought I'd say this, but I sure do miss that stupid train whistle coming from the bushes. I would put up with that whistle forever if we could just have your dad back."

I lost track of Sue after my parents passed away and their house was sold. But I think of her often, when I hear a train whistle, and smile at the memory of my dad hiding in the bushes waiting to attack. The inheritance from my dad wasn't society's predicable property and money, but rather the richness of being a character and the zest for making ordinary living a gift to be savored.

Catcher of Dreams

By L. J. Shook

Have you ever wondered where that one special gift comes from that causes one person to be an Olympic Champion and another to become a Criminal? I think it is the ability to dream. An Olympic Champion seems to have a well-defined dream that has been recognized early, encouraged and supported by family, friends and teachers. Not one young child, when asked about their dreams, has ever said to me, "I want to be a criminal or someone who grows up to do drugs and bad things to hurt other people and myself."

Usually, children's dreams are of doing heroic deeds, fighting the monsters of the night and the bad guys of the day. It's only after hope and dreams are lost, altered, or forgotten by adults or people in their lives that a child becomes something other than what they have dreamed about. Can you imagine the effect we could have on our future and the future of our children by spending the time helping one child, one teen, or even one adult to believe in their dreams? If we could all have one person in our lifetime to help us catch and hold onto our dreams what a difference that would make. A Catcher of Dreams that would recapture all our hopes.

Surviving the moment plays such a big part in raising children that sometimes we forget, as parents, how important it is to believe in the future, and our dreams for the future. Paying the bills, working long hours, feeding and clothing our children and providing shelter takes a huge toll on our lives. In the chaos of living, we forget to dream, and we forget to teach our children to dream.

If we don't teach our children how important it is to have

dreams for their future, then who will? Do we really want the autopilot of life to choose our future and your children's future?

Regardless of your age it is never too late to start dreaming. There isn't a day that passes when an opportunity doesn't present itself to believe in your own ability or someone else's. If all we can give is one word of encouragement to another or an opportunity to believe each day, then it can be enough to make a difference.

My dad was a wonderful loving man, and I couldn't have asked for a better father. But he never once asked me what my dreams were for the future. I don't think he ever knew my dreams. He had dreams because he painted beautiful pictures of the Wild West, but he never talked about his dreams or asked me about mine. It was always assumed that I would get a job, marry, and have children. Those weren't dreams they were just assumed duties that girls my age always did.

When I was a senior in high school I wanted to join the Peace Corps after graduation. My parents' signature was required on the forms. My dreams weren't taken seriously, and my mother even ridicules my dreams. When I needed guidance and support the most, no one was there. I didn't share my dreams with anyone and never let myself become vulnerable again. After a while I quit believing that dreams could come true and I went on to do the duties that girls my age have always done, job, marriage, and children.

Secretly I still had dreams, but they were buried deep. In their place I had wishes like, "I wish I would win the lottery. I wish I had a new car. I wish I had a new job or made more money." Deep soul dreams were covered over by shallow surface wishes. People didn't make fun of you when you wished. How could I have dreams that would require believing in myself, and that had not been taught to me nor something that I believed possible.

A few years later, while working at a Radio Station, it was my job to arrange for a speaker to talk on our call-in program. While talking to the speaker for the next day's program I was asked some personal questions about myself and my dreams. There was hesitation in sharing such a vulnerable part of myself, but he had a nice voice and was three thousand miles away. I would probably never meet this person, so it was easy to tell my long-ignored dreams to a stranger on the phone.

Total surprise came when he gave encouragement to me and valued my thoughts and dreams. He even spoke about such matters in a way that caused me to believe that dreams were an important part of living, necessary even. This nice man I now call my mentor has continued to encourage me with phone calls, information and his wisdom. He was a total stranger that changed my life because he took time to give encouragement to a fellow human being. His gift of, "giving me back my dreams." has been one of the greatest gifts I have received.

One of my dreams was to be a writer and another was to paint wonderful pictures. Several of my stories have been published and I was even an editor of a magazine for beginning writers. Ribbons that have been won hang next to the pictures that I have painted and entered in local art contests.

My seven-year-old grandson shares my love of art and by my side he painted a picture this past year and won Grand Champion for his buffalo painting. His picture and name were on the front page of the local newspaper.

Think about your dreams and ask other people what they dream about. Because without dreams we wouldn't have music, art, movies, books or a trip to the moon and the list is endless. Just stop and think of all the things we have and live with daily that required a dream to make it happen. We would never have had electricity, cars to drive or any of the luxuries that we have today without a dream behind them to get it started.

My catcher of dreams didn't enter my life until after my children were almost raised. I, like my parents before me, hadn't taught my children about dreams. How can you teach something that you do not know yourself? But it's never too late to make a change, and never, never too late to have dreams. Today my adult children and I share our dreams, believe in each other, and give constant encouragement.

In doing the things you love you demonstrate courage, self-respect, and self-worth, setting an example for others to follow. All of us can remember having dreams sometime in our lives. If we were lucky, we followed our dreams, but others have lost our dreams along the way.

A dream standing alone, without action, is not enough to see it fulfilled. A future without dreams leaves us nothing to look forward to...plan for...live for...die for. Without dreams life loses its joy, its passion, its spark, and its reason to continue. A life without dreams needs alcohol, drugs, and violence to cover up the pain of not being heard. Dreaming is the difference between living and existing. A person can never get too old or be too young to have dreams.

The United States has more people willing to help catch dreams than any other country in the world. What a great thing it would be if this world were full of people willing to catch each other's dreams. If we all had a goal to stop and catch a dream or two for ourselves and someone else what a huge, long-lasting gift that would be.

I know for sure you can change your life, alter a family and make a difference with every dream you catch.

Courage

By L. J. Shook

This story isn't about me. It is about a person who has touched my life, changed my course, and made a difference to the person I choose to become. I only enter this story because I want you to know that people and their actions do affect our life and possibly our future.

Most of the time we feel like we are ordinary people whose lives bump up against other ordinary people without knowing or recognizing anything exceptional about one another. The closest we get to a real hero is to watch them on TV. Fame touches our lives, on an artificial level, through our interest in Sport Heroes and Movie Stars.

Rarely do we get to meet a famous person or a real hero, the kind of hero the world talks about anyway. But I personally think that meek and ordinary people do exceptional acts of kindness and courage all the time that go unnoticed and unfortunately unheard. Sometimes we touch a life and change a course and go unaware of the ways and means we have affected another person.

This is a story about a friend who is in no way ordinary but has been forced to live an altered and less than ordinary life for the past eight years. My friend's name is Harrison.

Harrison has had a few health issues, and his doctor referred him to a clinic in St. Louis. Because of his health problems Harrison asked someone to go with him and assist him on the journey from Cincinnati. This visit to the new Clinic could provide Harrison with treatments that would be life changing and life altering for him. It was a big deal.

The first appointment was canceled because the airport was fogged in. A second appointment was made and as it approached his excitement and anticipation grew. Harrison did what he does every day he read his bible and prayed about the journey and the outcome. A day before the second appointment the person who had agreed to assist him on his trip called and canceled. A lesser person would have been devastated or mad and started grieving the loss of such an opportunity. They would have accepted the conditions the world was trying to force upon their life...but not Harrison.

When Harrison went to bed that night he prayed as he always does but ended his prayer that night with; "If you're not going to this appointment God then I'm not going."

The next day Harrison got up and prepared for his journey. Sometime during the night Harrison had decided to go on his trip to St. Louis alone. The reason this decision was such an extraordinary one is Harrison is quadriplegic and paralyzed from the fifth vertebrae down and the clinic he is going to is the same one that Christopher Reeves went to.

I was Harrison's home health aide for three years and have been his friend since. I know the care and help that is needed by Harrison every day. I bathed him, combed his hair, dressed and undressed him, emptied his catheter, strapped a fork to his hand so he could eat and helped him brush his teeth and lowered him into his wheelchair. I have assisted him with all the things that are needed for a person to get ready for bed or get ready for his day.

All the freedom to move that we take for granted every minute of every day are not freedoms for Harrison. I have helped Harrison and know firsthand the hardships of managing a wheelchair and luggage. The problems of getting him transferred from his wheelchair to his chair lift, lifting the wheelchair over the stair rails and then getting him back into the wheelchair again to just get out of his house.

The difficulties of getting him onto an airplane into his seat and back off the plane again are daunting. The long walk, escalators, trains, and shuttles that were needed to get to the boarding area at the airport. This is tiring for an ordinary person but almost insurmountable when trying to push your own wheelchair with paralyzed hands. I know the almost impossible task of trying to get Harrison and his wheelchair into an ordinary car when a van with a chair lift is not available. I understand what it is like to negotiate steps, too-narrow doorways and opening and closing doors that for the ordinary person isn't even thought about but requires much thought when your body functions in any way different from the norm. All the little things we do automatically have to be dealt with in a different way from the perspective of a wheelchair.

The reason I am telling about my friend was the act of courage it took for Harrison to step out in faith when he was unable to even take a step.... had me awe-struck.

Harrison started his journey by calling a few friends to come and help get him out of the house. But from the time he entered the van that took him to the airport until the time of his return home it was a relay of God's ordinary people helping my friend to his destination. There were twenty-one ordinary people one right after another mysteriously showing up when someone needed to push his wheelchair, get his plane ticket, and manage his luggage. Helping Harrison on board and off, to eat, to go to bed at the hotel and get up in the morning. Preparing him, helping him, loving him along the way to his appointment and then back home again. Twenty-one of God's ordinary people made a choice to help a stranger when they saw that someone needed a helping hand. No time during his journey was Harrison without someone ready to help him.

Do you think that any of the family and friends of those twenty-one people knew that their family member or friend had been a hero that day? I consider their kindness an act of a real hero.

Harrison received good news at the clinic. With therapy his chances are good at recovering some mobility again. But the journey was as exciting for him as the destination. He knows that with God's healing, his chances are even greater. Harrison has prayed for a total and complete healing and believes it will happen.

I know that Harrison will keep God to his promise, and I wouldn't expect anything less from a National Champion in Kick Box Karate with a roomful of trophies to prove it. Harrison was trying out for the Olympics at the age of thirty when he was kicked in a National Competition that broke his back and paralyzed his body from his lower neck down. My friend understands more than most what it is like to fall from fame and become meek and less than ordinary in the blink of an eye. But I consider my friend one of the most extraordinary people I know.

Thank you friend for showing us an outstanding act of faith and what true courage is all about and giving so many ordinary people the chance to become a hero, even if only for a day.

Dare to Be All You Can Be

By L. J. Shook

When you leave your physical body and go to meet your maker, can you joyfully say; "Every mistake that I made was mine. Every error in judgment, flash of genius, act of kindness or hurtful deed was mine. Everything that I incorporated into my life was by my choice. If you can't say those words then maybe you haven't been living your own life but imitating the people around you.

Wonderful creativity was used to ensure that every one of us turned out to be an original. Even identical twins and triples that come from the same egg are still different enough to be their own unique self. With such great effort made on your behalf why would you want to be a copy of another person?

Once I worked for a Hospice and during this time I nursed and nurtured patients who had all sorts of terminal illnesses and were in the final stages of dying. Without exception, the patient who took full responsibility for their choices, whether good or bad, died easier, quicker and with more peace. The person who had spent his/her life pretending to be something other than their original self was forced to face the reality of their illusions and had a harder and more prolonged time of dying.

Sometimes it felt like the Universe was holding up a mirror for them to see the original person they had been when coming into the world, not the illusionary one they had lived their life portraying. For some hospice patients they would endure endless weeks of hard suffering before coming to terms with the way they had lived and loved. The patient that hadn't lived an original life would do everything possible to postpone that day when they would be seeing their life review. That one moment at death when we all see the things we have said and done and how our actions have affected our life, and the lives of those we touched around us.

One Halloween my oldest daughter took my grandson Trick or Treating. They had to search several stores before finding the right costume my grandson wanted to wear. With a flashlight in hand, new costume and a plastic pumpkin to haul home his loot of candy he was ready. They canvassed the neighborhood for goblins and candy. Several blocked down the street they approached a neighbor dressed like a witch sitting in a rocker on her front porch. As my daughter and grandson approached, the witch let out a loud cackle and said, "Come here little boy...I like to lock little boys like you in my garage." Another scary cackle came as she stirred her cauldron of candy. Without hesitation my six-year-old grandson moved forward bravely collecting this treat.

My surprised daughter asked her son, who had trouble sleeping in a room alone, "Zach weren't you afraid?" Zach puffed out his chest and replied, "I'm Batman, Mommy! Everyone knows that witches are afraid of Batman." Zach wasn't brave because he was being himself, he was brave because he was Batman for the night and everyone was afraid of Batman, in the eyes of a six-year-old.

How many of us wear our Batman, honest employee, good parent costume? Do we fake being a nice person when we aren't really all that nice? Is the person reflected on the outside the same as the person on the inside? Is your image a product of all the choices you have made and everything you want it to be? Or are you someone who has let other people think for you, choose for you, lead you because it was easier to follow a group, the crowd, or another person, than stand alone?

A friend from high school had a son the same age as one of my daughters. At the age of twenty-seven he was still living with his mother and putting no effort towards becoming independent or a man. When he was in high school he was wild, in a rock band

and did a lot of things he regretted, like drugs and drinking. One day he decided that his life was lacking something important, so he joined a church and spent the following years leading a good Christian life which was as opposite to the rock band as possible. The problem was that he did this with at the same level of extreme as he had done with his rock band years. Last summer he went into a stress center because he was having trouble dealing with life and his feelings of anxiety.

At the time he was working at a video store and living with his mother. He didn't pay rent, buy groceries or worry about utilities. There wasn't even a girlfriend in the picture at that time to cause extra expense or added worries. My thoughts were, "Gees oh Pete, how much stress could he have living in his current protected and sheltered conditions?"

This young man's physical stress came from trying to force his creative spirit into the rigid and very limited space he had created from his religious beliefs. Instead of using his religion as a source of strength and direction he had used it as a place to hide out. He had become fearful of being found out or making past mistakes in the eyes of his religious peers. So, he didn't live, move forward, set goals or plan a future because he was afraid to fail. His stress was his soul crying out in pain because he had taken a beautiful, talented spirit and forced it to be an imitation instead of allowing it freedom.

I once took an oil painting course. At the beginning of class I had made an error in my perspective and spent the rest of my class time trying to paint over the mistake. The more I painted the muddier the colors became. I couldn't cover up my problem and I didn't know how to fix it. The teacher watched my struggle and finally at the end of the class period walked over to my easel. She asked me if I needed help. I said, "Please, can you fix this?" Without a word she took her palette knife and scrapped my entire hour's worth of work from the canvas. The art teacher then said to me, "That should help."

I just sat there and stared. I wanted her to fix my problem not wipe my canvas clean. Where the canvas was once white now stains of color remained but my original error in perceptive was gone. Now all I had to do was correct my past mistakes and start over.

So many times, I have compared my life experience to that piece of canvas. Our life is like a picture we paint, if it doesn't suit us, or we don't like what we see then we need to scrape off the mud and start over. The stains of our past will still be on the canvas, not as a punishment but as a reminder of where we lost our way. We can change our perception and create a new picture. We were given all the tools we needed at birth. Our canvas of life can have any color, scene, or people we want. It's our choice.

When your last days on earth are approaching will you be able and willing to have the canvas of your life spread out for view and say, "It's all mine, flaws and all, but it is my life's picture created by me." Or will you be feeling the pressure of your fake imitation, "It's not my fault, that person made me do it. I didn't know it would turn out like this. I was just following the group, the crowd, the news, that line of people. I just did it the way everybody else in the world was doing it. My friends talked me into it. The drugs caused me to do it. I was drinking and couldn't help it."

I think that every mistake we make is a lesson learned, every failure a boundary established, every hurtful act towards ourselves or another is part of our character being built.

Somewhere, in our soul we know what a divine creation we are. We need only to acknowledge and set free that deep spring of bliss that feeds our uniqueness.

You were created with love and intelligence to be a one-of-a-kind original. Dare to be... all you can be. The world needs the unique beauty that only you can create.

Dare to Be

By L. J. Shook

Dare to be a sparrow at my knee
A colorful blossom in a tree
What do you want to be?
We all need to decide on a course to take
Accountable for all the decisions we make
What's your dream...What's your goal?
Life without focus will take its toll.
Doctor, lawyer, beggar man, thief,
It's your choice, your thoughts, your belief.
If you could choose anything you see,
What would you pick...what would you be?

Ebony Man, Black Sister, My Friend

By L J Shook

Oh sister, brother, friend with ebony skin
What are you doing, where have you been?

Your journey was long, arduous with time.
Where is the ladder you struggle so hard to climb?

Too much violence over hundreds of years,
Bows my head, fills my heart with tears.

Inherited shame inflicted on Jews, Indians and Slaves,
Ancestral blood of white-washed deeds flows in our veins.

What is done to one is done to all,
Why can't we understand this higher call?

Black /White children all hurting, killing, in pain
A legacy of sins visited from ancestral shame.

So much striving, colored man, to be equal to white,
It has corrupted you to be prejudiced, and full of strife.

You have copied your persecutors lessons well my friend,
Justification, reasons to hurt another...violent trends.

Where is the difference? What have you learned?
Why hasn't your suffering caused a contrasting turn?

Forget the lies of inferiority the past has sown,
Remember God's promise and what you have always known.

Creative seeds of greatness are your right.
You are divinely connected and full of light.

You are loved, courageous, beautiful and strong,
Remember your true heritage and set free the wrongs.

All your struggles and suffering weren't for naught
Teach us... help us to learn... a new course to be taught.

Ebony man, black sister, my friend,
It's time for a better way, it's time to begin.

Eeegads Fifty-Three!!

By L. J. Shook

A customer with silver hair is a fairly, routine occurrence in my job as a cashier. But the face attached to the patch of white-grey hair caused me to do a double take. It is a face that has floated in and out of my life for the past fifty-three years. Fifty-three years...eeegads. I don't feel old enough to have known anyone for fifty-three years. Come to think of it, I didn't even know my own parents for fifty-three years, both passed away before I had reached that age.

Anger flashes through my body when Silver Hair laughs at my double take. He calls to me, "Hey Shookie," while he waits for me to take care of the customer in front of him. He is not surprised to see me as I am to see him. I work the graveyard shift, 10pm to 6am, and no one accidentally sees me at that time of night or morning. My younger co-cashier tells the gentleman with silver hair that she would be glad to wait on him. But he rejects her offer and replies, "No thanks. I've known this cashier since kindergarten, and I need to harass her."

Harass, irritation and a hundred other annoying adjectives clog my mind with another spurt of temper. Why is it that the people that make you feel good about yourself stay in your life for fleeting moments of time, yet the pain-in-the-ass people stay forever?

Fifty-three years, that number bothers me, and I can't understand my strong reaction to Silver Hair this time around. Maybe it's the fact that after all these years of knowing someone I expected or at least hoped for more than irritation and being harassed.

Ole Silver Hair has always been able to find me, even when I moved out of state for ten years. It's like he hovers on the edge of my life and makes sure that I still exist without being interested enough to know the details on how life is treating me. His actions are not that of a stalker, he is more like a quick-dancing boxer, jabbing punches before jumping quickly away just like he did in kindergarten. A technique he learned in school and has never outgrown.

I have sixty plus years of living that have knocked off my hard edges and polished out my thoughts, my rock's hard edges have been smoothed by life. Meditation and prayer have brought me so many answers, but none seem to fit with Silver Hair. My studies into self-help books have helped me understand everyone, but this guy. The unresolved issues seem to be on his side of the fence and not on mine. His only claim on me now is that we went to school together from kindergarten to graduation.

Silver Hair has stacked fifty-three years, one against the other, without wanting to be anything in my life other than a person who irritates.

I want to punch his nose, rattle his little pea brain hoping he will finally understand that he has had a wonderful opportunity to have a good friend, and he has been such a buffoon that he has missed it.

Silver Hair finally makes it to my cash register with his purchase and a smart aleck grin on his face. What goes around really does come around. He is, at least, forty pounds heavier and I smile, not because of his grin or joy in seeing him, but because of his puffed-out exterior. He is a lot heavier than in the past. All those years of him telling me how much he dislikes fat women, of course anyone bigger than a fashion model would be a fat woman according to his rail-thin, bones-sticking-out standards. Good ole Karma has staked a claim on him. It couldn't happen to a better person.

"Why are you in town?" I asked Silver Hair.

The jungle drum, in the small town where I live and where

we grew up, had beat out grapevine information that he had moved to Missouri and married again. His first wife divorced him after she went to the stress center. Just stating the obvious.

His wedding ring catches the light as confirmation, and he replies,

"I'm here for acupuncture. I come back to see the doctor that I like."

The faint light that has shown through the door as friendship slams shut and I know no more information will be forthcoming. I want to ask him if he is happy being married and tell him how glad I am that he has found someone to spend his life with. I want to know how he has been doing since his bad car accident. Fifty-three years should allow more friendship information than what just happened. I could get more details about a person's life from a total stranger.

Not once did he ask, "How are you doing Shookie? Is life treating you well? What's new in your life? Are you married? Have you written that book?" Something...anything that might resemble a normal relationship with a person I have known for so long. But the door of communication is closed tight.

What a waste!!!! Silver Hair turns and waves goodbye over his shoulder as he makes a quick exit through the side door, in a hurry to escape. Why bother? What is his need to keep hovering on the edge of my life to just irritate?

The whole interaction bothers me more this time than all our encounters in the past. My young co-worker notices my frown and asks.

"Was that man your Teacher in Kindergarten?"

I laugh out loud and dance a couple of steps trying to imitate the young kids. All my anger dissolves. My co-worker, who is younger than any of my children, is shocked and laughs out loud at my unexpected behavior and ability to dance.

Well, at least now with Silver Hair's new robust figure he should be easier to spot him when he comes lurking around the edges of my life. I have decided I no longer have the urge to punch him in the nose. There is way too much violence in this world already.

Instead, my wish for Silver Hair is that **all** his chickens come home to roost; because he would, as sure as life, be in trouble, it would put in danger his closed-down mind and buttoned-up emotions and that would place him at risk of becoming a normal human.

What are the odds of that happening after all this time? You never know! Life continues to surprise me even after... eeegads, fifty-three years!

Expectation!!!

By L. J. Shook

Expectation disguises itself as hope,
a stealer of dreams and ways to cope.
It gives promises that it will not keep,
binds our choices, causing us to weep.

Expectation hovers over everything we do,
Using broken dreams... disguised as new.
Distorting reality as a daily rue,
twisting lives, so we have no clue.

Expectation's victory is our loss,
pretending to be savior and a boss.
Expectation is a like a bad dream,
a terrible habit or a wrong scheme.

Expectation is a kiss with promise.
A lover's tease that is not honest.
A night of passion and hopeful bliss,
the next day forgotten without remiss.

Expectation uses magic tricks with skilled illusions,
forgone acts of deceptive conclusion.
It sweeps us up to soar among the clouds,
then drops us to our knees, so we cry aloud.

Expectations by nature can never be true.
It does not allow freedom of another's view.
A one-sided perspective, a self-absorbed vision.
It is a selfish and limited person's provision.

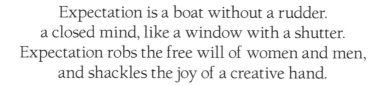

Expectation is a boat without a rudder.
a closed mind, like a window with a shutter.
Expectation robs the free will of women and men,
and shackles the joy of a creative hand.

Expectation is not a prayer, a goal or even a dream,
Its only power is a controlling scheme.
It can be a cruel taskmaster inflicted by others,
Or a self-induced punishment that always hovers.

Joy, free will, and God's love,
Are the blessings needed to rise above?
Unconditional love will set you free,
guide your spirit to what it is meant to be.

Joy can flow through your fingers like bits of sand.
Only you have the power of your heart, mind, or hand.
Make your own choices with conscious endeavor,
and seek divine love... that will last forever.

Family Thorn

By L. J. Shook

I went to a funeral today, my uncle, mother's only brother. Out of six girls and one boy there are only two left now and one has been diagnosed with cancer. Three funerals this year, one by one they leave us. It makes me feel the loss of my own parents even more. My parents have been gone for years. It is strange when your parents pass away how some part of you feels like an orphan. I was a grandmother in my own right when my last parent, my mother, passed away but I still felt like an orphan once she was gone.

Any family gathering on my mother's side has always left me feeling rejected, with the lonely title of 'black sheep' firmly etched on my forehead. Whether this label was earned by me or attached to me by my mother's lying I will never know for sure. Maybe some of both, after a while a person will act out the behaviors of the labels that have been attached to them. This seems to happen without determination of thought or purpose of action. It just happens. Maybe it is because, after a while we begin to believe the labels that have been assigned to us and automatically our behavior becomes the label.

In the past, part of me felt the hurt from these labels but there was always another deeper part of me that embraces the fact that I am different and do walk to my own drummer. It doesn't matter anymore. I have had the labels so long that the family has trouble letting go of their old mind-set regardless of my growth and life choices. The blessing of maturity is that I no longer care about the labeling. In a way it has freed me to become the person I always felt like I was on the inside not the person that everyone expected me to become.

Most of the people that believed the labels are dying off

and leaving their families, my cousins, in their wake. I am the oldest girl born in a family of sisters on my mother's side. This was probably the first of many reasons for the tension between my mother and me. My mother was the one who sought her mother's approval the most and received it the least, 'The Family Thorn.' I guess part of me does understand the disappointment my mother felt giving birth to a daughter and bringing the first granddaughter, another girl, to a mother who thought, 'being male allowed you freedoms and concessions that females never were allowed to experience. Being a female in my mother's family was just another ordinary, burdensome, occurrence.'

Mother's three sisters who were born before her managed to have a male for their first born. Being the oldest girl with so many younger cousins caused me to be the official family baby-sitter in the large family of my mother's sisters. I have changed the diapers of all my younger cousins at one time or another except for the older boys. The cousins remember me fondly even if their parents had other thoughts colored and generated by my mother.

I have always felt that in the pecking order of the family clan, my mother and her family held last place. I was never sure what caused me to have these feelings. It could have been that we had less money than everyone else or the fact that my mother was the 'family thorn'. All families have one and my brother and I were the lucky or unlucky ones to have, The Thorn, as our mother. It was probably the combination of the two that held us to the last run of the family ladder.

The baggage that comes with being The Family Thorn is generally passed onto the children. Our one saving grace was that our father was well-loved and respected. The thing about a Family Thorn is that she wasn't born a thorn but developed into one because of the way her family treated her. She was the middle child, three older and three younger siblings, and the one born next to the only boy. The perfect slot for being ignored.

I have always felt my parents held the last run all these years until my uncle's funeral. I realized that we may have had some company in that last slot, ironic really, when you think about it. My uncle was the only boy born to my grandparents and was treated like a God by his mother and his six sisters. The status of, 'male child,' seems to be a huge thing in my mother's side of the family clan. I think all the family spoiling him truly did spoil my uncle, and negatively affected his future for being a good man. And his family's stain of dysfunction was evident for all to see at his funeral.

Being the child of The Family Thorn had an upside and a downside. The downside is that not a lot is expected of you in the way of achievements. No one believes you will accomplish anything and therefore you don't believe in yourself enough to even try to strive for anything important. That is the curse of the whole thing, a self-fulfilled prophecy that you will never really amount to much in this world. The upside to this curse is that you don't have to live by the standards of the family. If nothing is expected of you then you can make your own rules and live your life without a family standard of performance hanging over, you.

I think that having no one to believe in you is the biggest sadness of all in family dysfunction. You are not taught to dream big dreams or set bigger goals or push yourself to the next level. Whether we like it or not, most of us only live up to the expectations that are set and influenced by the people around us. That standard of not being, 'believed in', does leave a stain for all to see. The many levels of family dysfunction can generally be boiled down to the common denominator of, 'not having someone to believe in you,' affects the way you process feeling loved. This can start from a small thing like not being taught to achieve, to the huge overwhelming things like sexual trauma or abuse, where you weren't believed in enough to be cherished or protected.

On the family's dysfunctional meter our family probably holds a moderate middle ground position. We have a few closet alcoholics and weed smokers, still functional and hardworking, but all needing a crutch just the same. Nothing on the hard end of the meter, mostly just social and emotional cripples passing on their family traits. In today's world and on the evening news, sex, drug or other horrors of abuse are reported nightly. Our family is closer to being functional than dysfunctional, but it could be because the world's standards have slipped so low. Each time I see the family I realize that regardless of our family dysfunction we keep on going and growing and that is our reward and gives us the glue to remain a family.

Maybe the belief of a perfect family is just a fictional idea anyway. We are all limited and struggling to reach the standard of how we believe a perfect family acts. The problem is that everyone has a different idea of what makes a perfect family. Possibly, the real answer is...there are no perfect family...only the family that we were given to work with and learn from, and maybe that is our curse and our blessing in this lifetime, but most of all they are the ones that teach us our lessons, good and bad. It is up to us to learn the lessons and grow beyond them, so we are not a thorn for our own children and family.

It's okay to know a Thorn or even be relative to one, but more important just don't be one.

Family Thorn

By L. J. Shook

A family Thorn is the one you love to hate,
They push and prod and continue to bate.

They are our bruisers of feelings,
and the bearer of harsh dealings.

Everyone has one... I'd dare to say,
a stirrer of the pot of intense dismay.

Sometimes related... sometimes not,
either by blood or a married into slot.

Thankful when not of our gene pool but married in,
wondering how and why they became our kin.

Some are born trouble and others are taught.
They know how to hit all the sore, soft spots.

It is hard to think of them as teachers,
when they act like critical preachers.

They test us, stretch us, and expand our boundaries,
They infuriate, offend and madden us soundly.

Yet the Family Thorn teaches us what no one else can,
tolerance, forgiveness, and enough back bone to stand.

The next time you encounter your Family Thorn... just grin,
they are doing you a favor... teaching you how to bend.

Fingerprints We Leave

By L J Shook

All of us have lived long enough to have watched hundreds of TV programs that involved crime, murder or other acts of violence. One of the first clues looked for to solve the crimes is always the gathering of fingerprints and other forensic evidence.

Over the years forensic science and medicine have expanded and grown into very serious and complicated tools to solve all sorts of crimes, and the medical field is now able to detect and diagnose illnesses and understand the origins of diseases.

What this has taught me is that we are all more connected than we realized, and all our actions, touches, and words have far more importance than we could have ever imagined. This happens on many levels, spiritual, physical, emotional and mental. I believe the effects of personal interaction we feel on these levels whether positive or negative can change the chemistry in our body and alter our ability to fight illness and disease in a natural built-in God given way. I don't think we were originally designed to handle and process the levels of stress that we encounter in today's world. Not to mention the chemicals and toxins that permeate all aspects of our lives now.

When we interact with someone we leave our emotional fingerprints on that person in the same way that we would leave any physical fingerprints on a doorknob or surfaces, person or things we touch. If you think about all the things you touch in an hour, or a day, it boggles the mind.

In the same way criminals need to take care of the fingerprints they leave at a crime we too should be forever mindful of the emotional fingerprints we leave on family, friends and all the people we encounter. The question to be ask is, are you leaving loving fingerprints on the people around you...or other kinds of fingerprints?

One person comes strongly to mind. He was one of my patients while working at Hospice. This man was bed-ridden and unable to walk or talk. He was fully conscious and understood everything that was said to him but was unable to answer or move. You could tell he understood by the alertness of his eyes. He had to be fed, washed and fully taken care of by his wife and all the hospice nurses and aides that came to his home. The doctors were unable to diagnose his illness or disease but were all in agreement that he was dying.

He was as vulnerable as a newborn baby. You can imagine my dismay, when helping his wife change the sheets on his hospital bed, she started to be exceedingly rough with him, sometimes pinching, poking and occasionally smacking him. I kindly tried to intervene and told her I would gladly change the sheets myself without her help. But she refused. I quietly eased my way in front of the wife, but she went to the other side of the bed and continued to treat him roughly. His eyes showed his concern and discomfort.

I wasn't sure what was happening to her and was afraid the stress of taking care of her sick husband long term was affecting her mind. I went around the bed and hugged her shoulder and quietly talked her into letting me finish with her husband.

This couple did not have 24-hour hospice care, so she was on her own with her husband for all the hours in-between hospice visits. After my patient was taken care of I went and sat at the table with his wife to talk to her. I started by asking her about her husband's illness and how long she had been caring for him and how long the nurses expected him to live. The wife fully understood he was dying and how weak he was. I kindly asked her why she was pinching him and hitting him.

It was like a damn broke and between the anger and the crying the full story of her marriage came tumbling out. Her entire married life she had felt weak and vulnerable, and her husband had physically beaten her, emotionally abused her, and mentally degraded her. She had never felt strong enough to get away from him, so she had endured thirty years of his abuse and now she still was not able to get away from him and was saddled with the burden of caring for this man she hated.

I knew I was way out of my element and ability to change the situation in this home. Part of me believed the patient's condition was God given and maybe some form of retribution for his life of inflicting abuse. The wife's behavior was a reaction from thirty years of crushing fingerprints that still bruised and imprinted her mind, and spirit, and affected her emotions daily. I felt that some part of the wife was so damaged from all the years of abuse that she could barely help herself when she pinched and punched the dying husband.

The wife and I talked about kindness and forgiveness, but her heart was hardened towards her husband. Nothing could be done during the time she was alone with her husband, when no one else was there. One tiny part of me wanted to punch the husband myself for all his years of brutality but it was a fleeting second of human nature trying to get into my mind. He was dying and vulnerable like a baby; how could a Godly person give him anything but grace and kindness in his dying state regardless of the legacy he left in his lifetime?

Later I talked to the nurses about the wife and other care givers had reported the same conditions that I was upset about. Our office was sending a counselor out to talk to the wife and give her some much-needed mental support and help.

Nothing could be done about removing the husband from the home because the wife wasn't inflicting enough damage to really hurt him. This was a financial situation that couldn't be altered and in my thoughts a God business situation. Thankfully I was only assigned to this patient a couple of times and within a few months was informed he had died

How much of our behavior is created and affected by all the fingerprints that we still carry in our mind, emotions and spirit from the people we have encountered while living and moving through our life?

Just think of all the men that have come back from war with PTSD and the way they are affected, sometimes for the rest of their years. Note that this condition is called post-traumatic stress disorder, not a disease, or illness not even mental illness but a mental condition by a traumatic act imprinted upon someone.... or performed by someone, that profoundly affects their life and thinking to be forever changed.

Deep bruising, life-threatening, scar-like fingerprints imprinted upon emotions, in the worst way possible. As in war there was always a purpose, a cause, a reason for the war and things done in the name of war. And yet even with the best cause, purpose or reason our warriors come home broken, physically, emotionally, and spiritually. Broken physical conditions can be healed or can be adjusted to quicker than the spiritual scars and open emotional wounds that still linger.

Since none of us are perfect and will all agree that there are times, in all our lives that we have been mean, unkind and even have hated a person or a situation, based on the way we were hurt by them. So many of our children may suffer from less than loving home conditions and now emotional abuse from their constant media connections that we don't understand and have trouble even checking on. Every one of us, regardless of our age, has had at least one situation in school that affected us so badly we still carry the scar from that incident.

I think it is important, and becomes more so every day, that we are consciously aware of all the fingerprints we leave on the world, the people and life around us.

Remember your Fingerprints touch everyone and everything.

Fingerprints aren't just left on people but also the environment, society, and animals. A pit bull can be a best friend and protector or become a vicious mean attacker; both ways of thinking and nature of this animal are determined by the fingerprints left by conditions and people around this dog when growing up.

All fingerprints are not destructive or hurtful. I think most fingerprints are loving and kind and do lift a spirit, a thought, a mind, a heart, a condition, an environment...a life.

Each day is an opportunity to choose the kind of day you want to have, the kind of person you want to be, the kind of fingerprints you want to leave in the world. So many of the physical fingerprints we leave are done without conscious thought; please be conscious of the emotional fingerprints you leave today when you touch another person's life.

Flat Stanley And Kolton

By L. J. Shook

Dear Kolton,
I opened my mailbox and what did I spy?
A letter from you, with Flat Stanley inside.
Stanley was peeping out all folded and crunched,
I gave him a Reiki treatment which helped him a bunch.
He ate some of your favorite dessert and his stomach grew.
He started to swell up and I thought he'd turn blue.
We took a trip to Cutler to see Adam's Mill.
Stanley had so much fun he couldn't sit still.
Next Stanley went to Rockville and took an Art class.
He painted a picture and had a blast.
Then to the covered bridge where the water ran fast.
He threw rocks in the creek and made a twig raft.
On to Lebanon and your favorite park,
with swings and slides and dogs that bark.
Back at my home we played games and he's glad he won,
except when he was Old Maid, then he stuck out his tongue.
He made bookmarkers for his teacher to use in class,
to help her mark assignments and keep on task.
Flat Stanley is tired; he has had such fun,
but he misses his buddy and playing in the sun.
Stanley hugged and kissed me, and said, "Good-Bye."
I felt so sad...I wanted to cry.
He promised he'd visit another day,
Maybe the next time, when you come to stay.
Flat Stanley hopped into the envelope for his trip back.
So, he could come live with you, Kolton, in your backpack.

XOXOXOXOOOOXXOOOXOX Love Grammy

Fried Egg Brain

By L. J. Shook

I was coming home after my computer class and my brain felt like a fried egg sandwich. You know the kind where the egg was fried too hot and too fast, and it has brown crispy parts around the edges.

My plan was to get a few things at the store, go home, take off my shoes, snuggle under my fuzzy blanket and take a nap so my brain could rest. I pulled into the parking lot of the store and spotted a couple of places to park but by the time I got to the first one a car had pulled in already. I headed for the second space and the car in front of me got it.

My jeep circled the parking lot trying to find a space close to the building. At my age energy is like gas in the tank and you only have so much to run on, so finding a close spot becomes a priority. I spotted the perfect spot and headed for it, but a white car driven by an old woman and passenger came towards me and was weaving around. Frankly, I was a little scared to get too close until they landed somewhere so I hung back and waited. Of course, they landed in the space I was headed for. Dealing with three lost spots with a fried brain was not good for my stress level.

My doctor advised I change my ways due to health issues. So, on my journey to better health, I discovered I needed to give up stress. I have been working hard to let go of anger, judgements, being critical and ego.

Like an old hen who gets her feathers ruffled when mad, I started to feel my feathers fluff up. I circled the parking lot again and found a place closer to the building, it was one space up and across from the old man and woman that had cut me off. I chided myself on the need to get fluffy and how, with patience, it all turned out better.

When I turned off the engine, I noticed that the old man had gotten out of the white vehicle and was pacing beside his car pointing at the ground then at the yellow parking line and then at the front of their car. I smiled and the hurry I was in evaporated as I watched the old couple. When he got back into the car the old woman jumped out and soundly closed her door. She stood mutinously off to the side with her black granny purse clutched to her chest. She shivered when the chilly wind blew her hair but stood her ground with soldier-like intent.

Being an old girl myself I have experienced a few mutinous stands during my life. I chuckled and appreciated her thinking. Then she looked up and I was taken back. Her face, as my grandma would say, looked like she had been sucking on a lemon. My thoughts were, "Oh Boy! That is not good."

The old man got out of the car and came around and opened the driver's door and got in, neither of them spoke. He backed up and pulled forward a couple of times and finally pulled the car in space the way he wanted it, not necessarily better than she had it. When he got out, I looked at the old woman's face again, all I could say was, it looked like she had started on a second lemon. There was no need for words because the body language was speaking volumes. It appeared that this couple had been having loud conversations without speaking a word, for many years.

The old woman started walking to the store and kept three feet between them. I had another chuckle and thought, I think marital bliss has fallen off that marriage.

With a smile on my face, I said a little prayer. "Thank you, God, that at the age of 75, I have the freedom to park where I want and the way I want, without censorship. I am gloriously free to have my own thoughts and say what I think and do what whenever I feel like when I feel like it. This wonderful time in my old age gives me much needed space to grow more, criticize less, and chuckle in place of getting fluffy. I so appreciate that I am no longer chained to the big boulders of time, duty, money, or job, and all the heavy responsibilities of family are behind me."

"And PS God, I really thank you that I don't have the need for an old man husband like the woman in the white car."

Gather Together

Christmas is here and all through the land,
We gather together with friends and clan,
We put aside differences, we put aside greed,
We share and care and do good deeds.
A year of war, a year of grief,
Has opened our heart and helped us speak.
About wrongs that need to be put right,
or things that have caused us to be so uptight.
The meaning of caring has taken new depth,
And we remember for all those we have wept.
If only we could remember the whole year through,
To do as we know in our spirit and not as we do.
This is my Christmas wish and my prayer,
That in all the months coming you will show you care,
Each person willingly gives all the grace he can spare.
Bless each one, whether friend or foe,
To think all are enemies, that is our woe.
Gather together with out-stretched hands
And spread love from mountains to far distant sands.
May Christmas be a spark that glows all-year,
As we come together against prejudice and fear.

By L.J. Shook

Gittin' Her Wind

By L. J. Shook

On turning fifty I lost my cool,
But soon realized it was my most precious tool.
Half-century age marks slowly encroach.
Creaks and pain signaled the approach.
Bags, sags, wrinkles and lines,
All signs of someone past their prime.
TV commercials tell me I'm old.
But menopausal attitude frees me to be bold.
Society teaches, I have become weak.
No longer a breeder, no voice to speak.
Convinced by Mother at her knee,
Women, my age are winter's tree.
Old and barren, in the twilight of youth,
Well, my friends, here's the truth.
Universal mysteries now unfold.
So many life experiences yet to be told.
No toddler hands pulling me down,
or a husband's censorship and controlling frowns.
More dangerous now, than ever before,
empowered, experienced and so much more.
World of commercials, limits and labels,
You can have your prefab fables.
With borders, boundaries, barriers to bend,
This old girl jest' getting' her wind.
Fear of negative opinions no longer scare.
Frankly Scarlet, I JUST DON'T CARE.
Opportunities to teach and love abound,
So many lost, weak, misguided...just look around.
So, stand aside, I've experience to lend,
This Old Girl Jest' Gitting' Her Wind.

Grammy This is Commando!

By L. J. Shook

Our time was at hand; protect the command center at all costs. A final check of equipment was needed before the Mission Commander could begin. Two black mini flashlights substitute for walkie-talkies. Into the Commando's black mission bag goes binoculars and a small battery-operated radio, standing in for the Commando's radio center. One kaleidoscope via spyglass telescope and one adjustable pencil eraser substitutes for the sophisticated spy equipment of an eight-year-old. Last, but not least, (the grey tiger cat) Rain's, sponge balls, are commandeered by the Commando's government to be used as hand grenades. With all his equipment intact, the Commando is ready for his mission.

"Here Grammy!" says Commando. I'm handed one mini flashlight /walkie-talkie so I can be in constant radio contact with the Head Commander. The mission, if I choose to accept it, is to take the garbage to the basement without encountering the enemy, secure the laundry and recover vital supplies: a two-liter bottle of pop from the car. After supplies have been secured, we then do a reconnaissance mission from the back of the apartment building to the front to intercept important communications, (the mail) and circle back to the command center without procuring heavy losses.

"I'm ready Commando," I speak into the bottom of my smooth, black, pretend, walkie-talkie. "You scout ahead for hostile forces while I let out our highly trained, attack cat and put this cookie dough in the refrigerator."

"Roger, over and out." The blond head of my soon-to-be-nine-year-old grandson nods as he answers.

Old knees creak and pop as I slouch down and slither along

the back stairwell to the shadowy basement. It's hard to tell which is creaking louder, my left knee or the steps. Musty air drifts up from below with the promise of spider webs and multi-legged crawly things. Commando and attack cat are leading the way. With my body pushed up against the smooth painted wall, in my best spy imitation possible, I hug the corner and start down the last set of steps. What I wouldn't give for a Dick Tracy trench coat and an Indiana Jones hat.

The back door of Apartment One swings open and my young neighbor looks at me, with a strange and startled look. I lift my head and give her my best cheesy smile. Her look communicates to me that I have crossed that invisible line between normal and other. I have gone from the presumed normal, old, fuddy-duddy who lives in apartment three to that place where Twilight Zone music is played. I can even hear strains of the music start to play in my head. Commando calls me. "It's all clear Grammy."

There isn't time to salvage my reputation. Our mission is at stake. Commando and the attack cat depend on me.

The highly skilled, killer tiger cat takes charge of all gray enemies that are low, fast moving and mousy. The Commando darts in and out of shadowy corners and large appliances while my hands work fast to gather the clothes from the clothesline. We are a trained team working together for the good of the mission. Commando retraces his steps to take the attack cat back to headquarters. I darted out the basement door into the hot, sunny parking area. Exposure to imaginary enemies quickens my retrieval of our vital supplies from the car.

The recovered provisions are added to the top of my already full arms of clean laundry. Commando slips from the basement with a loud click of the door and proceeds with his reconnaissance mission up the driveway to recover our top-secret communications. Commando turns back and asks Second-In-Commando, "Grammy, can you hold this? I need both hands to check out the landscape with my binoculars."

My arms are full and juggling to position the two-liter bottle of pop as one hand gains freedom from beneath the pile of laundry to accept Commando's sophisticated equipment of special radio and grenades. His walkie-talkie, spyglass telescope, other assorted and necessary spy equipment sticks out of every available pocket, an old black purse stuffed full hangs from his neck as a spy bag. He looks like a combination Saturday morning cartoon character and SCI-FI Alien standing before me and I can't help but smile.

My feet struggle to find balance on the incline of the driveway. Mission orders are to follow the Commando in his effort to secure our top-secret communications. The warm texture of the red brick building registers through my "Grammy Means Love," Tee shirt while hugging the wall with my backside. This grandma's body must exert extreme effort to live up to my rank of Second-In-Command. The reality of being a pack mule alters my darting, and spy-like moves.

"Commando, I could use some help here. The enemy is going to capture me if you don't help carry some of this stuff," I whisper loudly.

"But Grammy, I need both of my hands to hold the binoculars," Commando whispers back.

I remember this! I can see the logic of a nine-year-old male still works in the same way it did when my brother tried it out on me forty plus years ago. A little mature, female, reasoning was needed to help this mission. "Commando, if I get captured, the enemy will get the supplies and there won't be any soda for the command center."

"Okay, Grammy," sighs the Commando heavily. "What do you want me to carry?"

"Why not take back your spy stuff and scout ahead so you can open the door for me," Second in Command answers?

Commando reclaims his equipment and stuffs it all into his black purse/commando bag, then silently slips along the building, darting between bushes and the driveway. The front of the apartment building is soon secured along with the top-secret communications/mail. My feet trudge along supporting the burden of our spoils-of-war. In his best commando fashion, my grandson scouts the remainder of the steps until we are safely back, in the second floor Command Center.

Ice clinks in the half-full glass of pop as it is set on the table in front of the Commando. The back of one tanned and slightly dirty hand wipes the moisture from his lips. "That was a good mission Grammy. Can we do that again?"

"Can I use the top-secret, laser/eraser pencil next time?" The Second-In-Command asked.

"Okay, Grammy," Commando sighs as he eyes the freshly baked oatmeal raisin cookies cooling on a plate in the middle of the table. "But I'll have to show you how to use it, "cause" you might accidentally shoot your foot."

"Zach...I mean, Commando, I need someone to taste test these cookies, just to make sure that nasty spy, Zoloft, didn't sneak into the Command Center while we were on our mission and tamper with the cookie dough. Do you know anyone brave enough to take on that mission?"

Commando sits tall in his chair and grins up at Second-In-Command.

"I can Grammy. I can!" Second-in-Command smiles back and kisses her brave Commando next to the oatmeal raisin cookie crumbs on his cheek.

Grandma Was No Ordinary Woman

By L. J. Shook

Grandma was a divorce woman at the end of the first World War and in those days being divorced was not the norm and only talked about in hushed tones even though my grandfather was the one that found someone else.

My grandmother was never an ordinary woman. She was independent, owned a business and was self-supporting before I was born. She lived a few miles away in Indianapolis and ran her own beauty shop but when her father got sick she left it all behind and moved back to the family farm in Illinois, to help take care of him. Once he passed away she stayed there alone, ran the farm and has lived there ever since. She went from living in a city with her own life and friends and maybe a boyfriend, and most certainly modern conveniences, to living on a farm with electricity but no running water and barely any neighbors. All the water used for cooking, dishes, cleaning or laundry had to be pumped. The perfect job for an eight-year-old, or so they told me. The wash house was a building beside the pump and all laundry, and baths were done in the wash house. Any warm water needed was heated on top of a paraffin stove and an old wood stove was used for heat in the winter to keep things from freezing.

Grandma raised chickens for eggs, meat and pin money when she sold extra eggs. She ran a rural country beauty shop out of her kitchen and big wooden barrels with cheesecloth over the top were kept by the back door to collect the rainwater she used in her beauty shop. Rainwater was different from regular water and made your hair soft and shiny. Grandma had regular customers, giving permanents and doing those flat waves against your head thing, she did with her fingers. I see old time pictures of women from long ago that had those waves in their hair.

I used to sit on her stool upstairs and pull back the crisp starched curtains made from feed sacks covering the wall of shelves and just look at the beauty of all those jars of canned fruit, and vegetables along with jellies and jams that filled her many shelves. This was grandma's security and food for the winter.

All the colors, shapes and sizes of filled jars were seen through my eyes as a work of art. I even understood, at the age of eight, the hard work it took to fill all those jars because I had helped her with some of it.

My grandmother didn't drive so she was as self-sufficient as a person could be and only depended on neighbors when she needed to go to town for items she couldn't grow or produce herself. Grandma had a party-line phone with an ear thing you had to hold to your ear and a little handle you turned when you wanted to call someone. I remember Grandma's number was, three long and a short, turns on the crank. I can't always remember where I park my car, but I can remember that.

One thing I remember most was my grandmother's whitewashed, three-hole outhouse. My grandma was an artist, and I contribute this part of her personality to the reason she had a three-seat outhouse with linoleum on the floor, along the seats, and flowers planted around the outside of this white pristine outdoor building. Only an artistic heart would ever think of such a thing. She had the nicest outhouse in three counties or so I heard the old biddies say when getting their hair done. Grandma took great pride in the rarity of her facility. Anyone who came to visit wanted to see this highly decorated building whether the call of nature was upon them or not. It looked like one of those sheds in a modern decorating book.

At the young age of eight, I didn't find it weird that three people could use the outhouse at the same time or would even want to. I was glad that someone was with me, so I didn't have to be by myself. At home in Indiana, with a regular toilet, I didn't have to worry that I would fall through the hole, like Alice in Wonderland, and end up in a strange world or place. Or worse, that snakes lived beneath the holes and would jump up and bite me when I couldn't see them.

One summer my older cousin and I went to visit Grandma for a week. We were weeding her huge country garden when I needed to use the outhouse. Grandma asked my cousin if she would take me. As we were sitting down to do our business, we looked up and saw a big snake resting on the ledge above the door. My worst nightmare had come true. Snakes **did get** into the outhouse. The only way in or out of the outhouse was through one door with the snake above it. This wasn't just a little old green garden snake either but a big black full-grown snake, or at least it looked full grown to me.

My teenage cousin talked to me quietly and told me to hurry. It would be important for me to remain calm. She instructed me to go out the door first, not look up, leave the door open and run like crazy. We both made it out of the outhouse okay and went and told grandma.

My grandmother did the bravest thing I have ever seen. She knocked that snake down with her garden hoe and didn't stop chopping until the snake was in little pieces. The outhouse was dinged up and we had to get bucks of soapy water to wash away all the snake blood. My older teenage cousin helped grandma by sweeping up all the black snake pieces. Eck!

Grandmother hated snakes as much as I did. But I learned that summer how to be brave and that sometimes you must do things you don't like just because you may be the only person who is available to get the job done.

When I asked grandmother about the outhouse being all dinged up and whether she was sad, she smiled and said, "I guess, little girl, 'Pride Go-eth before a fall.'" It took me a few years to work out the meaning of her words but like all good lessons one day I understood what she told me.

The outhouse was never the same again and left in its banged-up state. I guess to remind Grandma about the lesson of pride. I was never the same either, but I learned several valuable lessons from my grandmother's example that summer. How to have courage even when you are scared because someone younger or smaller needs your protection, and you can handle any situation if you make up your mind you can do it. These lessons have been imprinted on my life and taught me the true meaning of courage and how it was done.

My father's mother was the one person who showed me how to be strong and true to myself. How to take what you have and make it look the best regardless of how humble or limited the funds, even the lowliest of places like the most common places like an outhouse, can be made to look beautiful. If creativity is in your soul then anything can be made into a work of art.

Some of the best parts of who I am were taught to me by a grandma who chose to live her life outside the box, and the word ordinary just didn't ever apply to her.

Hard Day of Dying

By L. J. Shook

Taking that final step into the next dimension is the last act we do as a human and we do it alone. A rattling noise comes from Della's lungs letting the world know that in this natural process of dying, another organ is trying to shut down. Gasp... rattle...rattle...gasp...rattle...rattle sounds fill the room.

Like a dog, hot and panting in summer heat, her breathing is fast and shallow. Air that is pulled in sharply through cracked dry lips that barely reach her lungs before slowing to rustle and rattle its way back out. Gasp...rattle...gasp... rattle...gasp...rattle.

I must make a conscious effort not to copy my patient's breathing as I sit in my state of vigilance. Moving, stretching my back, shoulders, and arms to break the tension that has settled in from the long night. Every part of me hurts from the energy pumping through my body in readiness to deal with the dying that never comes and adrenaline that is never used. A year's worth of experience working for Hospice, and dozens of patients, tells me that the next breath could be her last.

Della has spent months dealing with her hideous enemy of cancer, an enemy that has taken everything, and has left nothing in return except a ravished, broken shell where a healthy vibrant body once lived.

Being surrounded by family and friends may give support during the last few days of life, but in truth the only way a person can die is alone. But in any case, dying comes hard. It's not like in the movies where a person lies in a white pristine bed in a state of sainted glow. The perfect timing of family and friends floating in to give their last flowery proclamations of love and appreciation before the soon-to-be angel takes a last, easy, earthly breath. The truth is that most of my patients die during those few seconds and minutes when no one is watching... and choose to do it that way. Hand-held loving vigilance prolongs their death and seems to inhibit their spirit from passing freely to the next life. It is easier for them to slip away without the pull of love from family standing guard.

The dying person is not an angel or about to become an angel. They are human beings that have lived a life of good choices and bad judgment like the rest of us. For the most part, the family will be hard pressed to remember enough memorable actions to talk about at the funeral. Tending to repeat a few special experiences that happened during a whole life lived well. Usually, a person's life is defined by two or three acts that stood out during their lifetime and these all will be repeated among family and friends during the viewing and service.

Dying is not a pretty, clean, odor-free or pain-free experience. Dying with a terminal disease comes hard...on the body, on the patient, on the family, on everyone involved. Dying is real, profound, natural and as necessary as living.

Another rattle is added to the already unnatural breathing. This is the breathing of near-death, a warning, a hovering of spirit between this life and the next. Usually this end-of-life breathing only last minutes, sometimes an hour, sometimes more, but never in my experience as a Hospice Aid, has a patient had the death rattles for days on end, Gasp...long pause...rattle, rattle...gasp...long pause...rattle, rattle.

Pain comes from my chest, reminding me to breathe. I have been unconsciously holding my breath, because the breathing of my patient has changed yet again. Even with her death rattles she seems to be breathing better than I am. This night goes on forever. No one can hold this intense level of anticipation without feeling the strain. Members of Della's family started dropping in their tracks after the sixth day of their mother's death- rattle breathing. Like trees in the path of a lumberjack's saw they have fallen, emotionally, physically and even spiritually. My mind wanders to the family spread out all around the house, sleeping on couches, on the floor and in other rooms. This is their first full night of uninterrupted sleep in six days.

Weary from the months of care they have already given their mother has left them exhausted with no reserve of energy to deal with this latest twist of events. Months of Hospice, with social workers, and nurses teaching them how to nurse and care for their mother have prepared them emotionally for this final stage but it's the physical side that can't maintain the duration. They are ready to let her go. Every unspoken thought of love has been placed into words every loving act of kindness has been given. The preparations have been made for weeks just waiting until the time is right. Now is that time for the final words to be written on the last page of the life-story named Della.

Compassion for the family added hours to my already daily visit of bathing, changing and preparing Della for her day. I need to think of her as patient, keep them all patient in my mind or I can't sustain the passing away of a living, loving person week after week, which is all part of my job.

The book that I brought to help pass the night slips from my fingers. No author's attempt at artificial living can hold my attention after seeing the true reality of dying. I want to know what this real person looked like before cancer carved her into the skeletal body that lies before me? Was she a good person, what were the things about her that set her apart from other people? Did she push her family to the edge of endurance in living as she is doing in her dying? My eyes search the walls and dresser tops for a picture of her former beauty. I want a hint of her personality, a glimpse of a woman's life, how it was lived and whom she loved. Gasp...long pause...rattle...long pause...gasp...long pause... rattle...long pause.

The sun's glowing fingers slip through the blinds at the window and another day nudges out the night. Stretching as I stand and move to my patient, for my hourly tug on the pull sheet to roll my patient over into another position. A soft moan interrupts the gasp...rattle... gasp...rattle. My patient straightens her leg. The movement is painful and causes her to take a deep breath, the only deep breath she has taken during the ten hours of my shift. The haunting eyes of the deathly ill look up at me from the bed and a spark of life shines though. A person, more dead than alive, watches me as I lean in closely and whisper, "Good morning, Della."

A soft look is all her energy level will allow and it passes for a smile. A Gasp and rattle came from her open mouth. I kneel by the side of the bed and moisten her parched lips and open mouth with a cold damp cloth and slip ice chips gently into her baby-robin mouth as I have done all during the night. Sometimes a patient becomes alert right before the last few breaths. I circle her left hand with mine while my other hand strokes her forehead and face with gentle fingertips of compassion. Love slips out from under my armor, and she becomes the one thing I have fought hard to prevent... part of my family. She is so sick... so vulnerable.

Sometimes I think coming into and going out of this world are the two hardest things we do as humans. I move closer and asked, "Did you want to say something Della?" She squeezes my hand and a large dose of adrenaline surges through my body preparing me for my job of waking her family because she has passed or listening to the last precious words of a dying patient. Della's raspy voice is stronger than I expected, and she pulls all her energy together to whisper a question, "Could I have a cup of coffee?" A soft laugh ripples through me and splinters my tension into a million pieces, I reply, "You can have anything you want Della."

My overnight shift has come to an end. My patient has been bathed and changed with all her medication given and she is now resting in a clean bed with an untouched cup of coffee by the bedside. In her mind she still wants the coffee that has been her morning ritual for the past sixty-some years, but her body is unable to tolerate even a drink of water, much less a sip of coffee. I have prepared the coffee anyway hoping the morning smell of coffee will give her some comfort. Amazing how old habits and cravings still linger even after the body is no longer able to process them. The family is stirring and rested for the first time in weeks.

Della still isn't ready to leave this world, something is keeping her earth-bound. Maybe some deep dark secret, unexpressed act of love or hurt, important information that needs to be expressed that she has kept buried during her life and now it is demanding to be heard before she dies. Or maybe it is the fear of dying because so many of us feel we don't deserve to see God due to the way we have lived and loved.

I report to her family about her condition and her night and gather my things to leave and start my daily duties with yet another patient, like Della... like my father, who also died in the same way.

I tell my patient goodbye; the deathly rattles of my night continue into the morning as I leave the room. It looks like Della and her family are in for another hard day of dying ahead.

Postscript: Della lived another seven days after my all-night vigil, breaking all the usual hospice rules of dying, thirteen days of death rattles. My prayers go to the family members.

Not one of us is strong enough to fight that intensely, that long or that hard to live without God's help and a very serious purpose. The answer to this mystery will probably never be known, it is all between God and Della.

Here Fishy, Fishy... Here Fishy, Fishy

By L J Shook

Going fishing was one of my father's favorite hobbies. You could always tell when he was thinking about taking a fishing trip. His poles would be in a line and inspected while he sat sorting through his tackle box, to make sure all was ready. Of course, this was a hobby he felt all his children and grandchildren should know how to do. So, I was taught, to bait my own hook and cast out my own line. Dad did take my fish off the hook for me. I had a sneaking feeling this was more about not losing the fish than it was about saving me from the repulsion of the whole thing.

Even with my old cane pole I could catch fish, but for me it was about spending time with my dad rather than catching smelly old fish. Since I did'nt even care if I caught a fish, I was able to sit still and patiently wait for my bobber to move. When my son turned ten years old dad decided it was time for a fishing trip with his grandson and he rented a boat for the occasion so they could go to a bigger pond.

This is where the story gets a little sketchy. According to the storyteller, my son was having problems catching fish and my father had already caught a couple. Part of the problem had to do with the fact that dad was using better bait, and the rest was due to my son taking his line in and out of the water every five minutes. Unless a fish was really hunger and willing to jump three feet out of the water for a worm my son did not have a hope of catching a fish. Dad knew if his grandson started getting antsy and bored his fishing day would be short.

So, my father, the forever jokester, sat at his end of the boat and when he saw he was getting a nibble he would say, "here fishy, fishy, here fishy, fishy," and then reel in his fish. He talked my son into thinking that was the secret trick in catching a fish. While dad was helping my son with his pole he slipped the better bait on his hook, then they rowed out to a different spot. My son spent the afternoon using the secret trick of saying, "here fishy, fishy," and finally had the joy of catching a couple of fish. This secret trick kept my son busy and focused so dad could get in all his fishing time.

The two finally came home late in the afternoon, both sunburned, smelly, and smiling with a stinger full of large fish and tall fish tales about all the ones that got away. There was enough fish for our dinner and while we enjoyed our meal my son let it slip that the fish he and papaw caught were smaller, so grampa bought the stringer of big fish from a couple of other fishermen when they were packing up to leave.

On my father's face was his giveaway smile, he always gets the same smirky smile when caught doing his mischief. He chuckled and reminded his grandson that he was not supposed to tell that part of the story.

My son learned how to fish that day, spent quality time with his papaw and the most importance part of fishing ... learned to tell a tall fish tale.

It took a few years before my son figured out how his grandpa had really snookered him with the "here fishy, fishy," fishing tale he had spun that day. Dad always had his own brand of fishing.

Horse Fly on A String

By L. J. Shook

My relationships these days are pieces of what they once were. My friends now are a hogpog of leftover relationships from our earlier life. Now in our sixties we are mismatched and leftover pieces of the families we once were. We hang around, and bond together, in an odd sort of way.

We each have our story about our parents and grandparents to tell. The male in our group talked about his dad's recipes. His dad didn't have recipes for food but recipes for remedies. One such recipe was written down on a piece of paper he carried in his wallet. It included ground up aspirin, hot sauce, Ben gay, and a quandary of non-related substances that he would mix and rub on his body when he had pain. His father is now in his eighties and has no feeling in his hands and legs. We all surmised that the reason for his numbness was probably due to his home remedies he had applied all over his body for so many years.

My story involved my grandmother, a true countrywoman. Grandma lived alone for all the years that I knew her. My grandfather had been a veterinarian but had passed away long before I arrived on the scene. Grandma owned a farm, passed down from her father's side of the family that she rented out for income. Raising a huge garden was something she always did. Grandma canned and preserved everything for the winter. She made pickles, jam and jellies and all sorts of wonderful, canned vegetables. These were all lined up according to size and color on the shelves she had made in one of the upstairs bedrooms. On every visit I would raise the pristine starched curtain she had made to cover the shelves and just look at all those jars of canned fruits and vegetables. Besides being a joy of color and textures there was something comforting about having shelves of food just waiting for the winter season.

The last story came from our friend about her childhood and the family farm. She talked of the hard work, busy days and rarely getting to go to town.

She talked about how her blind grandmother would catch a horse fly in her hand. This was no small fete. Her grandmother would catch the horse fly and shake her hand to get the fly disoriented and then tie a string around it. When the horse fly came back to its senses, she would give her granddaughter the string and my friend would walk around the yard with the horse fly buzzing on a string.

We have collected the pieces of our lives and woven them together into the comfort of our friendships.

How Granny Scared the FBI

By L.J. Shook

When I was growing up, it didn't feel strange to have three grandmothers and only one living grandfather. It was the bonus plan. Grandma Watkins was our adopted grandmother and every bit of a part of our family like any blood-related grandparent.

My mind still pulls up clear images of Grandma Watkins: sitting in the yard breaking green beans with my mother, hemming my prom dress, or teaching me how to iron my first shirt for Dad. On the outside she looked like any normal grandmother, with white hair, starched printed dresses and black lace-up shoes that screamed, "For grandmothers only." She had a close resemblance to the picture of the grandmother on the cover of my, "Jan and Dean," record album. If she had lived in Pasadena, then I would have thought for sure, their song was written about her.

The first of her many curve balls she threw in my direction started at the age of nine. Think of my surprise when seeing someone with white hair, which I considered old, giggled like a schoolgirl. Her laugh was light, musical and invited me to giggle along with her. She taught me the true joy of giggling.

Grandma Watkins was widowed and had been a single woman for a long time before I came on the scene. Being widowed and descended from pioneer stock had made her very independent and self-reliant. She could do carpenter work as well as any man.

Most things about Grandma Watkins' personality came in sharp contrast to her little, old, granny, five feet one inch appearance. Her fascination with wrestling was one of them. She religiously watched wrestling on TV and would transform before my eyes into this short, animated spitfire that became actively involved in the wrestling program. While Granny watched wrestling, I watched her. She would jump up out of her chair, throw her arms around and coach her favorite wrestler. "Pin him down...Pull his hair...Jump on him...Gouge him," clicking her tongue she would ask me, "Did you see that dirty punch?" Grandma was always tired after her favorite TV program because she had physically wrestled each match herself.

My Grandma drove a little black Chevy Nova, back in those days the car resembled a box, and a big fluffy pillow was required for her to see through the bottom of the windshield. Her feet barely touched the pedals and shifting gears was a jerky and tense process. Looking to see where she was driving was done through the hole in the steering wheel. For the most part, it looked like Granny's car was driverless when going down the road except for her tuff of white hair which appeared above the dashboard. On a good day her driving would cause a grown man to sweat but as she advanced in years, she positively scared people off the street. Like any fiercely independent person her car was something she would not consider giving up.

A few days before the family conference was scheduled, on how to handle restricting her driving, Granny managed to get her car onto the interstate going in the wrong direction. Since Granny didn't know what to do, she just kept going thinking she would eventually reach a place to turn around. A full car of FBI agents, out of Indianapolis, spotted a car coming at them the wrong way on the interstate. Granny got scared when cars started coming at her and honking, so she pushed down on the gas pedal, and pointed the car straight ahead. The FBI seeing a car coming at them at high speed, which appeared driverless and was playing chicken with them, was enough for them to take to the ditch. With some difficulty they managed to get their muddy car out of the ditch and turned around. The agents went into full FBI pursuit. They caught up with the black car, pulled it over, and surrounded it with their guns pulled. Imagine their surprise when "The Little Old Granny from Pasadena," steps out.

The FBI wanted to arrest Granny on the spot, but she took them on in full, verbal combat and they backed down, instead they decided to call my parents to come and get her and her car. The agents canceled her license and made sure she would never drive again.

I always smile at my mental picture of my petite granny in a starched printed dress with a white collar and her black lace-up shoes standing toe to toe with all those tall, serious FBI agents towering over her. I often wondered what would have happened if the FBI agents had tried to arrest and handcuff her.

If they only knew all the wrestling moves, she practiced every week they might have been a little nervous.

How Well Does Your Attitude Serve You?

By L. J. Shook

It seems that we (collectively speaking) have developed a need to define our presence by our attitude. Saturated years of movies, sports, TV, and commercials have molded our minds and romanced our perception into thinking that only a strong, forceful and loud attitude will get the fastest service and the best results.

The weekend before the Christmas holiday, I took my car to have a wheel, and two tires replaced. It came as no surprise when I arrived, the waiting room at the tire center was full of people with the same urgency to have their cars ready for travel. I told the man at the service desk my needs and took a seat. Over the next couple of hours, I quietly watched and listened to the people around me. The long wait was not a hardship for a writer. Action was in full swing in the waiting room, and I was taking mental notes.

A thin sparrow-looking woman with sharp features paced nervously back and forth in the limited space. Taking turns smoking, doing laps or making caustic statements about her lack of, "On the Rim and Out the Door," service that had been advertised. An older, shrunken version of sparrow woman sat watching and nodding her head in agreement.

A grumbling man with beady eyes, whose protruding features and body structure resembled a mole, came into the store demanding instant retribution. He had paid an earlier visit to the tire center and the service garage had missed a hole in his tire. Now he stood pounding the desk loudly, ordering immediate service.

Mole man gravitated to sparrow woman like an invisible

magnetic force was pulling them together. The pair performed a ritual of smoking, pacing and complaining loudly, inflicting their attitudes on everyone in the room. Looking around periodically to see who wanted to join them in their dance of discontent.

Sparrow woman's and mole man's attitudes did not serve then well on this Saturday. Errors were made with both of their tires and the time to service them was almost as long as mine. They had come into the store expecting problems and their expectations were fulfilled.

As the room cleared a chill settled over the waiting room. At least sparrow woman and mole man had generated heat. Now only one other person remained. After a second shiver I asked the young man if he was cold. He was at the store center when I arrived, and his thin sweater didn't look warm. I was rewarded with a smile and conversation. He also sat quietly during the last two hours listening to the room of people. A flat tire the night before had put him in need of a new tire.

The desk clerk called the young man over and told him they didn't have the right size tire for his car. They wanted to put on a bigger tire than what was already on his car. This young man didn't yell or even become upset even though he had sat for the last two hours and waited. He quietly said, "I don't believe that would be the right size for my car. The desk clerk then gave him another option. He would sell the young man four new tires at a rate of fifty dollars less on each tire. The young man looked at me and smiled. Our shared smile was an unspoken bond of knowing that our attitudes had served us well.

As for me, I am not a mechanical person and know nothing about cars. The little I do know was forced on me by my son before he left for the Marines. One day he found me in the driveway, standing over my car in latex gloves with a kitchen funnel trying to pour oil down the dip stick hole. I was very irate that some man had designed such an unreasonable way to put oil in the car. As my son unscrewed the oil cap he agreed with me, in a very sarcastic tone, that pouring oil down the dip stick hole was very ill-logical and that's why a man didn't design such a thing. He next made me put fluid in my radiator, check my air filter and find the carburetor. Lastly he wouldn't leave me alone until I could prove to him that I could change one of my tires.

All this mechanical knowledge didn't help me one bit on this day because I didn't know anything about tires. So, before I went to the tire store I prayed God would bless the men that worked on my car and please make sure everything went well. I started out with the attitude that everything would go smoothly with my tire and my expectations were also fulfilled. I was also given an upgraded tire for the cost of less than I would have paid for normally.

Why is it that we expect so little from life, but we are so willing to embrace the misery and share it with others? I have yet to have joy inflicted on me by a stranger with the same intent or force as misery is so freely shared. Never has anyone inflicted two hours of joy and peace on me with the same level of exuberance that sparrow woman and mole man inflicted their misery.

The sharing of misery has become a multi-million-dollar industry. Misery is marketed and advertised daily. Just watch the trailers for the show advertisements for Jerry Springer and see the proof. Do you need the drama of misery and failure, or do you want quiet and peaceful results? Do you want performance, or do you need to perform? You can't have it both ways.

Are we so unaware of how truly exceptional we are that we feel it necessary to hang onto our misery so we can perform our little melodramas to validate our importance?

For your attitude to serve you best a conscious choice needs to be made between needing the credit of a deed or wanting results. It's the difference between feeding the ego or feeling the spirit.

Not too long ago I locked my keys in the car. I was returning some rented movies and managed to lock my door. My car was left running, and my spare set of keys now sits on the front seat of my locked car, in my purse. My radiator has been overheating so I am getting a little nervous. After trying all the doors with no luck, I stopped and took a deep breath. I pray, "God, it's me again. I need your help getting my door unlocked." God answers, "You know, Linda, I have had to add an additional Angel to your staff of guardians since you turned fifty."

With a smile, I went about helping myself until I could see what God had up his sleeve. One of the things I love best about God is his sense of humor.

The Staff at the video store were very nice, and one young man came out to help me. The window on the passenger side has been off track and sometimes slips a little, one of the few blessings of owning an older car. With his screwdriver we pried on the window, and it moved down smoothly like an invisible hand was rolling it down from the inside. Once the window was down a few inches the clerk put his arm in the opening and unlocked the door. Then he helped me put the window back in place. In the space of ten minutes, from the time I locked my keys in the car, I was on my way home.

I felt so joyfully blessed that I wanted to share my story with a friend. I told one of my friends the story of how I locked my keys in the car and the wonderful help that I was given from God. My friend didn't react to the story in the way that I thought she would. Instead of understanding the blessing and how my attitude to the situation had served me well she asked me why I didn't call the police or a locksmith to help. When I told her that I didn't need to she became angry and her answer was, "Well God just listens to you better than he does me." I wonder why?

I hung up the phone feeling upset about her reaction to my story. The next day I called her back. I wanted her to understand that God didn't listen to me any better than he listened to her, the difference was my attitude. I believe that I would be helped by the best means, in the shortest period, and the most effective way possible. Because that is how God does his/her work. I would have had to wait hours for the police to help me or for the locksmith to come and open my car. It would have cost me money that I didn't have. If I have waited on man to help me then my car would probably have overheated for sure. The difference between my friend and I, has always been our attitudes. I believe that all would happen in the best way possible with God's help. I go to God first for my answers and my friend always goes to man for hers.

My friend can do what she thinks is best for her.

As for me, I'm going where I feel safe, protected and loved. You can gauge the outcome of our decisions by the looks we have on our faces. I will be the only one smiling.

I Miss

Dear World, Just So You Know:

Another birthday has caused me to pause and think about all the things that have changed during my seventy plus years of living.

I miss that KINDNESS is now the exception and no longer the rule.

I miss TRUTH; it used to be a straight arrow. Now it is twisted, bent, and renamed to fake news to minimize its value and distort it true power.

I miss when name calling was done by children and punished by adults. Now it is the adults teaching the children how to be disrespectful.

I miss FAIR PLAY and HEROES; before coaches and mentors became sexual predators; when sports weren't businesses that had to win at all costs, and players set standards of conduct that didn't include drugs, guns, cheating and wife beating.

I miss HONESTY, back when you crossed your heart and hoped to die, stick a needle in your eye if you tell a lie. Today honesty is almost non-existent. Everybody lies about everything, and lying has become the norm.

I miss having GOOD LEADERS; men and women who tried to the do the right thing and want what is good for **all** the people, or at least gave us the illusion that was what they were doing. We don't even get the illusion anymore.

I miss when scandal and corruption were bad things with serious and life-altering consequences.

I miss, "One Nation under God with Liberty and Justice for all;" before the rich elitist made us into a polarity of people where justice for all is not available, and our liberties are sadly being eroded away.

I miss INTEGRITY, according to Webster, unquestioned honesty, uprightness, moral soundness, moral stature, principle, virtue, purity, decency, self respect, reliability, wholeness, strength, and **coherent soundness**. Have you run across anyone that lives at this level of integrity lately? I'm surprised they haven't petitioned to have this word removed from the dictionary.

Most of all I miss LOVE. I miss the time when love was a goal that everyone strived for and used as a gauge to value all things in life that were of importance. Now hate is openly preached, and we are battered daily with accepted acts of prejudice. Simple murder no longer has enough juice for us, now we have mass murders, serial killers, and weekly TV shows where multiple victims are tortured and mutilated for our entertainment.

Imaginary Lover

By L.J. Shook

Deep vibrating sounds play along my spine.
Imaginary kisses slid across my mind.

Thoughts of strong arms pulling me tight,
Caressing my body shadowed by the night.

Your voice resonates through my soul, and I sigh.
Words of love cross the distance and make me high.

A lover's touch, like no other man,
Caressing me with your voice but never your hand.

I sometimes wonder if you even exist.
Covering my body like the morning mist.

The rhythm of your song wraps around my heart,
Dispelling the distance that keeps us apart.

Just a country singer practicing his skill,
The love songs you sing take away my will.

I close my eyes and imagine you are real,
A flesh and blood lover that I can actually feel.

Whispered words of love brush against my ear,
Your lyrics hold me firm as you draw me near.

When time hangs heavy and the day slows,
Your voice is the music my heart wants to know.

Imaginary lover floating through the sky,
Singing tenuous notes of love that make me cry.

Just a country singer practicing his skill,
With songs of love you take away my will.

Deep vibrating music plays along my spine.
Imaginary kisses slide across my mind.

Imaginary lover singing your lore,
Invading my thoughts so I want more.

Kissed By an Angel

By L. J. Shook

Huddled in the darkened room of my parents' house, despair seeped into every cell of my body while reality takes its time and presses down hard. I had never felt so alone, or vulnerable. It feels like I am battered and abused... beyond value. The least bit of handling by rough hands would find me shattered and broken into a million pieces.

Divorced and a mother in my own right, I was very aware of how I had arrived at this place of desperation, at least my brain understood, but my heart hadn't quite caught up. How could giving back, to my dying father, all the love he had shown me as a child reap such despair? The irony was that I had chosen this course in my life. Putting my life on hold to nurse my dying father brings no regrets regardless of the high price I am paying. I am blessed with the opportunity to give my father the gift of knowing when he departs from this world he is loved and cherished by his only daughter.

A radio playing Christmas music drifts up to my second story bedroom, deepening my loneliness and hurt. This season above all others has a way of shining light on a person's life that doesn't quite live up to the world's fake and glossy images. Even the best of families has a hard time measuring up to these manufactured holiday ideas, but in a dysfunctional family the fractured parts seem to shine like broken glass when God's light shines on them.

Six months ago, my father departed this world, on the evening of Father's Day. It is appropriate, somehow, that such a wonderful father should pass away on a day set aside to honor fathers.

Since my father's passing, I have worked long hours trying

to scrape enough money together to escape this place that no longer feels like home. The tears continue to come. I don't want to spend one more day fighting for emotional survival. I have Given... Enough, the life of the only parent that loved me and the scattering of my own children during the last few months because there weren't enough hours left over in the day, after the yard, the house, the laundry, and the nursing, the cooking and helping my mother for me to be much of a parent to my older children.

Only for the sake of my dying father have I sustained the endless emotional and verbal abuse served up daily by my mother. My father's last words were an apology to me for enduring so much so I could take care of him and love him during his dying.

Dad was the one person who loved each and everyone one of his family, as we loved him. He managed to hold together this collection of dysfunctional people we call family. But without the influence of dad this Christmas season, everyone is floating away like pieces of wood on the out-going tide.

My mother's poor health, due to three open-heart surgeries, was the reason I moved back home to help nurse my father, but dad's passing has left my mother weak, angry and relentless. Her insults and criticism are like word-bullets she fires like regular target practice. It is mom's usual and distorted way of trying to ease her pain and vulnerability. Regardless of all the help I give her, disdain and resentment are my payment.

I pull the pillow tighter to drown out my sobs. The hurt and sorrow is so strong that it clogs my throat and impedes my breathing. With short grasping breaths I pray. "God...please get me out of this house! " I need to get away from this place, this room that is more of a prison than a haven.

I am so tired. "Dear Heavenly Father," was my whispered prayer. "Please forgive my weakness. Help me to not hate her, she is my mother, but I have nothing left to give. One more word-bullet and I will surely die. It feels like I have been alone for so long, struggling to be strong, trying to be both mother and daughter but I can no longer remember the sound of a kind word or the comfort from a loving hand. All I ask for this Christmas, Dear God, is to be held once more so I can remember feeling safe and loved again," was my prayer.

Noises drift up from the street and then fade into the background. The downstairs Christmas music becomes softer, more muted as I lay in this place halfway between sleep and reality. I snuggle closer to my pillow to muffle my sobs and ease the sharp pain in my heart. My eyelids slowly close, as the light becomes diffused and opaque. It was like I was drifting to a place of peace and love, where beautiful light and God's unconditional love is all around. A flutter of wings swished through the air as strong arms pulled me close and cradled me like a child. Gentle fingers touch the tears on my cheek and the stroke of a caress calms my spirit. The purest kiss is placed on my brow. The kiss opens my heart and mind to God's love and my own father's gift of sweet childhood memories. My heart takes flight and soars with the nourishment of such unconditional love. "Thank you, Heavenly Father," I whisper.

The Christmas Angel's visit was brief but answered my prayer with a kiss that set me free from the bondage of hate and the pressures of the world, to remind me once again of God's beautiful gift of endless love without conditions.

Lift us Father

Deck the halls and string the lights
Snow is coming... oh what a joyous sight!

Young children are excited and nervous as can be,
wondering if all their behavior, Santa really did see?

Winter mittens and colorful bundles of fleece,
protect, rosy cheek children, when noses sneeze.

Christmas trees sparkle, all dressed up for a reason.
Carolers sing songs and spread the spirit of the season.

Life is a roller coaster, giving us all a wild ride,
The gift of Christmas is a reason to put it all aside.

Lift us Father... above all our woes and strife.
Help us remember the sacred meaning of life.

Bless us... Oh God... and keep our families whole!
Clear our hearts and minds, so Love is all we know.

May Christmas bless you for another year,
And draw you close to all those you hold dear.

By L. J. Shook

Modern Man

By L. J. Shook

Oh man of modern ages.
Where is the wisdom of our old sages?

Regardless of your years or phase,
You chase beauty like someone crazed.

Your mind has been given the punch.
Programmed by TV to be one of the bunch.

The women in the movies you see are not real,
Just illusions of manufactured sex appeal.

The average woman can't live up to the test,
Of rebuilt beauties like Hollywood's best.

How well do you men think you would fare?
Standing next to Hollywood Hunks in the bare?

Beauty is body, mind and spirit...that is real,
Not silicone or faces carved by surgeon's steel.

Oh, how I miss a man that uses his own mind,
A man that can appreciate women of all kinds.

My Dear Joe

By L. J. Shook

Amber waves and twinkling blues,
A Smile with a dimple and whiskered red hues
Do you remember my Dear Joe,
Memories shared so long ago,
Of a sunny picnic under boughs of green,
with mossy grass and splendor scenes?
Quiet pond with rippling edges,
Shared kisses and tender caresses?
Two life-battered people enjoying new love,
You were my blessing sent from above.
Years long after that golden day,
A smile warms my heart, and my lips give way.
Memories surface of long, long ago,
And a red whiskered man,
My Dear Joe.

My Father's Garage

By L. J. Shook

My physical body looks at the rail thin body, hollowed blue eyes faded by pain, but with the eyes of my soul I see my hero, a tall man with brown hair. A loving parent that taught me to ride my first two-wheeled bicycle, bait a hook when fishing, plant a garden, and drive a car. The father, who carried me in strong arms when I was small, cheered my first feeble attempts at riding my birthday bike and doctored my bloody knee when I fell.

Memories surface when thinking of his eyes sparkling filled with merriment from the stories he told and the mischief he practiced. He had strong, loving, creative hands that could paint beautiful pictures, carve life-like animals from a simple stick of wood or fix almost any machine or engine. I loved my father with the closeness only a daughter has the privilege to experience.

Dad is the yardstick used to measure other men. His strength never wavered, and his courage only grew stronger over time. Dad's character remained true for all his seventy-three years. He was the one person in my life whose love never caused pain or whom I doubted. During the time cancer whittled away at his body dad accepted his fate and never asked the question," why me?" nor bowed to self-pity. I had never seen my father cry before, and the memory still pulls hard at my heart.

There were months of being bed-bound, with pain-riddled nights where only medication and the packs of ice loving placed on his body could lighten his suffering as we struggled through the nights. Never once did he cry or cry out. Only family members could do to him what, months of cancer, was unable to achieve.

My mother and brother decided they couldn't wait for dad to die before laying claim to his sanctuary, his things...his garage. This special space commandeered from his garage, where a car hadn't visited in years, but where dad's sanity and creative soul had resided during the last several decades. All of dad's treasures were housed in that garage, his tools, fishing poles, wood lathe and projects that still lay waiting for his touch and creative input. The garage was the place dad talked about while lying in his bed of pain. It was the one thing that gave him hope in his battle with cancer. It represented a future after a miracle would cure his disease and where he could pick up where he had left off, a promise that lay waiting for him, cheering him on.

With the sensitivity and forethought of a couple of garden slugs my mother and brother cleared away, hauled away, threw away and gave away my father's hope. Dad's skeletal body barely took up space in the hospital bed residing in the living room of the home where he had lived for the past twenty years and had chosen to die. Noises of my brother's and mother's activities carried in the window on the warm summer breeze, from the backyard. My father's hand clutched mine and eyes filled with pain spilled over with tears when dad asked me, "Why Sis? Why are they doing this?" Looking into the suffering eyes of my beloved parent was the hardest thing I have ever done when I answered, "I don't know dad. I don't know."

This thoughtless, selfish act took away dad's hope and added weight to his already heavy burden of dying. Dad's tears didn't lessen his courage in my eyes or waiver my respect of such a wonderful man. The goodness of my father didn't come from a single act of kindness or courage but from seventy-three years as a good man and forty years of being my consistent, patience and loving parent.

Dad died two weeks after his garage was cleared out. I still don't understand why my brother and mother did such a thoughtless act or what was so valuable in the garage requiring their greedy claim that couldn't wait until dad's passing. I do know that losing the dream of his garage took away my father's will and reason to live and shortened his life.

Occasionally I drive by the house where my parents lived for so long. The garage still anchors the corner of the yard, and I imagine dad standing outside with the door open, tinkering on his air conditioners and lawnmower engines or working on his woodcarvings. The was the place he could be found most days winter or summer, after his retirement. Regardless of their intentional or unintentional hurtful efforts to clear out my father's garage, they were not able to clear away his memories.

Dad was our anchor and the glue that held us all together and without his presence we had unraveled as a family. I don't want to forever hold the actions of that horrible day against them because part of me believes they truly didn't understand the hurt of their behavior. Which is sadder, the premeditated hurt done with forethought and malice, or insensitive, uninvolved hurt caused by limited thinking and greedy actions that come from someone who doesn't use their heart?

The legacy my father left me is the values that I hold dear and with those wonderful parental gifts I move forward and leave this sad commentary of the rest of my family in the past where it belongs.

Dad painted my life with the same bold brush strokes he used to paint his western scenes on canvases, and I will forever be blessed by such a loving parent...my dad.

My Right!

By L. J. Shook

Who do you think you are friend or foe,
to inflict your will and cause me woe?
Who says yours is the only point of view?
Maybe your advice is only good for you.
What makes you think you have the right,
to take my power and dispense your might.
Is your way so narrow and mind so tight,
that you can't see another's way, another's light.
Our Creator gave us all the freedom of will,
What are you playing at, when my wishes you kill?
Get out of my face... it's my say!
I choose no longer to be forced your way.
I'm tired of being your scapegoat,
when you want to bully and gloat.
It's my life...my thoughts... my day.
Leave me alone and get out of my way!
My choice...my will...my plight.
I'm fully accountable. It's my right!

New Boots for Carla

By L. J. Shook

The Group Home, where I worked as a Trainer, was located a few miles from town, on a narrow country road with no streetlights, sidewalks, and with an occasional house surrounded by large cornfields.

One of my many duties was to take clients to purchase clothes when needed. Carla, one of the eight residents, needed shoes. After dinner the second Counselor on duty stayed with the rest of the clients while I took Carla to town to get new boots.

Carla was a thirty-three-year-old woman who was mildly, mentally, handicapped, with cerebral palsy. Carla could walk without assistance but had a pronounced limp and needed to stay on even ground to keep from falling. Her life story was a sad one.

She was abandoned by an abusive father who didn't want to be bothered by a cripple, and she had suffered unimaginable abuse. Found by the police living on the street and eating from garbage cans, she was taken to a Protective Service Agency who sent her to our facility. Being a higher functioning resident, provided Carla the opportunity to work at a Handicap Workshop and earn money for special purchases, like her boots.

On the way home Carla sat in my front seat wearing her new fur lined boots and humming her contentment.

A couple of miles from the Group Home a loud thump comes from the right rear tire. The road was narrow, and snow was piled high on the brim making it difficult to pull over. The curve of road had a blind spot and was a terrible place to have a flat tire. I said a prayer as I tried to pull off the road. There were no lights to help me see and the closest house was too long a walk for Carla with her limited physical ability. I didn't want to leave her in the car by herself on that dangerous curve while I went for help.

I explained to Carla what had happened and asked her to stay in the car while I checked the tire. I had changed a tire before but not on ice and snow and I was a little concerned about the car slipping off the jack. I said a prayer for protection and assistance as I pulled the jack from the trunk. Out of nowhere a car appeared at the front of my car and a second one at the rear. Both cars left on their headlights and a man got out of each vehicle. The wind was blowing snow, and the dark night had a bite. The two men were friendly but spoke very little and proceeded to change my tire in record time. They worked like they had changed tires for a race car driver instead of being strangers. Both kept their heads down, and the blowing snow and their hats made it impossible to see their faces.

I thanked them for their help and asked if I could pay them, but they refused and were both gone as quickly as they appeared. I never saw the two cars approach in the blowing snow, and I didn't see them drive away.

A strange feeling warmed my heart and lingered as I stood in the whirling snow wondering what had just happened. I had a profound feeling the two men were guardian angels that had come to change a tire in answer to my prayer and keep us both safe on a dark winter night.

Old Age Birthday Poem

By L. J. Shook

Birthdays come at an alarming rate.
Saying, hurry, hurry, I can't wait.

Who needs the push... where is the rush?
Why can't they just slip by in a quiet hush?

When you were young and very small,
You liked the bang and clang of it all.

Now that there are more candles than cake,
It is a fire risk that you shouldn't have to take.

This is your special time to remember your life,
the good times, adventures, and even the strife.

All your living that has gone before,
has shaped you into the person we all adore.

Your gifts of kindness are a beacon in the dark.
Friends are bestowed with your love's gentle mark.

Celebrate your birthday, forget the number of years.
Blow out your candles and ignore the wind shear.

Old Tree New Branches

By L. J. Shook

I have never been one of those people that wore rose colored glasses. My view has always come from the, "Meet reality head on, place."

My views on life have been that we are like trees and if we are flexible and resilient then we can withstand most of whatever Life and Mother Nature throw in our direction. My artist spirit has been able to take what life hands me and enjoy whatever original piece of beauty life offers up.

I have a friend who always sees the best in everyone and every situation. Without this great view on life, she would never have overcome an aneurism, Multiple Sclerosis, or be able to walk normally with only the use of a cane to steady her. At the age of eighty she opened an Art Gallery and Bistro in her small town. The effects of the MS caused her to lose sight in one eye, but this hasn't stopped her from creating wonderful works of art that she sells. Her open mind and open heart have been an inspiration to all who get to know her.

This year I was forced to take one of my hard looks at reality when trying to find a different job. With unemployment holding steady at nine percent and the job market behaving like a bottle neck in traffic, my job search came to a dead stop. My present job involved more work added to more hard physical work with my pay barely above minimum wage. There was no increase in pay or even appreciation for the added work and it was fast approaching the new level of abuse that corporate American has been doling out to its employees, to maintain their same level of top-heavy greed.

I always thought that I would be one of those people who would work until a ripe old age. My plan was to keep moving so

I could keep going. I had seen too many men and women retire and then sit in a chair and watch TV until they dwindled away to nothing, physically and mentally. It was never my intention to retire, especially at an early age.

To me retirement was a dirty word. Job Fairs and other job seekers my age agreed there were no jobs to be found for someone in their sixties. With no husband to add income or support, the starkness of my limited options was harrowing. So, you can imagine my dismay when this hard-core realist had to face the fact that to retire early was my best solution.

I only told my family and closest friends about my retirement and didn't mention it to anyone else. I cut my hours at work to a few days a week and then over a couple of months eased out of my job completely.

When it was time for me to renew the lease on my apartment, I was forced to reveal my secret retirement. Word got out in my apartment building and then the dreaded invitations to play afternoon cards and bingo started to appear under my door. Ugh! I'm not ready. I don't have bottles of medication to talk about with all their side effects. I am not ready to enter the "One up Race." of my hip or knee replacement was worse than yours. Nor am I ready to get a cat or dog and the highlight of my afternoon is taking animals for a potty walk. I just can't go there. It is too much to expect from me. I haven't even adjusted to that awful word of retirement and all its ramifications.

My rebellious spirit wanted to feed my soul and not just fill up free hours, so I decided to take art classes from a one-eyed artist who sees things differently than most people and knows how to love life and enjoy all its beauty. For me this was a far better solution than pets, bingo and meds.

Art is a part of my family tree with my grandmother, father and mother all painters. I painted early in my marriage, but children and life all seem to get in the way of this pursuit. With all my new free time I now could take those art classes and pursue some of my abandoned dreams. My classes have taught me the beauty of trees, in my transition from occasional dabbler to everyday artist. I now see trees in a whole new light, all kinds of trees, nature trees and family trees.

I love the way the branches of a tree reach out for the sun, the way they stand strong through the years and show a new side to their personality with each new season. I especially like the trees that have branches big enough for adventurous tree climbers, children's swings, and can give shade to weary parents and travelers.

Retired people are a lot like trees and the true beauty of an old tree is it can still grow new branches. Having free time is the best thing I have done for myself in years. I have more freedom to come and go and enjoy my grandchildren. I am no longer tied down to a job I hate for my survival. Early retirement doesn't pay all the bills, but it does give me a steady income to build on. Now I can work part-time at a job that I can enjoy. I have time to explore life, people and new possibilities and grow new branches in any direction I want.

I still don't like the word retirement because its congers up an image of someone quitting and sitting at the back or on the sidelines and not participating in the ebb and flow of life. My life isn't ending; it is just the beginning, giving shade and strength to my weary children, setting examples and creating dreams for my grandchildren and showing the world just how much bloom, this old tree still has in her.

Old Woman's Cart

By L. J. Shook

Old women have been dragging their carts down the street towards home, brimming with groceries for years. We have all seen them at one time or another. Jokes have been made and comic skits are frequent on TV about old women and their carts. These are the old women with black sturdy shoes, and thick hose, that look like the old woman on the cover of my old Jan and Dean record cover.

So, you can imagine my cringe with I moved into a new apartment building for people that are fifty or older and the first thing I saw in the vestibule was one of those carts propped up by the door, waiting for its owner.

I refuse to be called an old person even though my age qualifies me to live in this apartment building; I'm just not ready to tote that label around with or without a cart to carry it in.

I held out on my resolve for a couple of months at least, until the reality of carrying my groceries from the parking lot, up the elevator to the third floor and then down the long corridor to my apartment changed my mind. By the time I reached my apartment I would have deep grooves in my hand from the weight of the heavy bags and usually I would need to make two or three trips back to the car or go to the grocery store several days a week to get all my supplies. Finally, my resolve fell away, and I asked my children to buy me a cart for Christmas.

Being a logical person won out over suffering for vanity. Once I embraced this stupid old woman's cart idea I realized that I had a work horse in my hands. Besides using my card for groceries, I use it to take my clothes to the laundry room, to move all Goodwill finds from my car to the apartment.

Most importantly it has moved my grandchildren down the

hallways in my apartment building and around the sidewalk to the 4th of July parade. With a cushy blanket on the bottom of the cart they could have their toys and a treat, and they were able to sit close to the street when the floats threw candy and were always safe from people bumping into them or having their view blocked when the parade came by.

It was a sad day for my youngest granddaughter when she became too big to ride in the cart. Most importantly my three youngest grandchildren all have fond memories of riding in my cart and when they were riding I wasn't running down the hallways and streets chasing after them.

Now other grandmas are telling me what a great idea I had and are buying carts to move their grandchildren around. It is a great way to manage those energy-filled toddlers with half the effort.

It is a good thing that Grandma's are smarter than they are vain.

Open Heart Surgery

By L. J. Shook

How many times will I have to do this? All her feelings bump and mash against one another, anger, sadness, resentment, and vulnerability. She hates this feeling of being naked and exposed. The feeling of family knowing where all those soft spots are located and using her defenselessness for sport, entertainment or just because they are not smart enough to know the power, they have over her...Family! We are at the mercy of our family from birth. The familiarity of knowing each other for so long and so well gives knowledge of where all the soft spots are hidden. It always shows when observing a family, how well they love by the level of respect the members treat each other's soft spots.

Sitting in the waiting room at Methodist Hospital, for Lera, is a well traveled road, anticipating the results of her mother's latest open-heart surgery, with family. Something they have done three times before. Lera feels vulnerable again, to all those planned and unplanned punches to old, unhealed, emotional wounds. It is always her by herself with her brother and his family. She is always outnumbered and alone with no one to give her support or get her back.

It doesn't matter how many years she has lived or how together she gets her life, as soon as Lera goes near her family she is pulled into a time warp. Conversion back to less than happy times surrounds her like a clinging plastic wrap. An old pattern of dysfunction rears its ugly head ...Dear God...its so much better to love them from a distance. The time warp is not so easily activated. The blows are minimized by distance.

Seven hours in the waiting room with her family has the worst of their dysfunction acted out and the tension eases, now she can remember why she loves her family, and not so much why she dislikes them. Only the anger remains. How can she feel love and anger at all the same time for the same people?

A Hospital Aide entered the waiting room with a solemn report on her mom's life and death struggle after seven hours in surgery. The aide says it will take two more hours, but their mother is doing as well as can be expected. She will be coming off the heart/lung machine soon. The end of surgery is in sight. An intense feeling of danger is unconsciously communicated and increases Lera's heart rate. The internal struggle begins, of wanting her mother to live but also wanting all the old conditions and patterns that cause so much pain and hurt, to die. How do you separate one from the other?

A little voice, Divine Guidance lovingly whispers, "Stand strong, move forward." Lera asks that deep down sacred spot, "What is causing the pain?" Answers dance around her exhausted mind. It all has to do with believing she was not loved, or worthy of being loved. Somewhere along the way Lera started to believe that she was defective and unlovable from all those years of acid-drip criticism by her mother.

Flashbacks of a four-year-old version of herself sitting on rough wooden steps at grandmother's house with tears streaming down her face dominated her thoughts. This was Lera's youngest memory of when it all began; sob after sob carries on the warm summer night air. Little fingers holding the back of her head where blond waist-length curls had been just a few minutes before, now only a very short bit of hair remains. All her beloved hair gone; the one thing she had cherished more than anything else as a child. Now after years of being a mother herself she wonders how a loving mother could purposely do such a hurtful thing to her child without an explanation or reason. Maybe that is the key to the puzzle. Having a loving mother who has faults is one thing but having a mother who is good and bad, loving and hate-filled in equal proportions is harder to understand as an adult and especially as a child. A mother is the one person in a child's life that should be trusted above all others.

Lera's mother had <u>promised</u> her that they would only trim a little hair off the ends, lies all lies. Something that she soon learned to understand would be a constant in her mother's behavior toward her. She remembers her grandmother confronting her mother later, after the haircut, when they thought she was out of hearing range. Her grandmother was a beautician, and her mother had talked her father's mother into cutting Lera's hair without her knowledge. The grandmother told her mother to never ask her to lie or help trick Lera again. The emotional scar was not from losing all her beautiful hair but was from losing a mother she thought would always nurture her and could be trusted. Knowing a mother is willing to lie to get what she wants even if it means hurting her only daughter is not something you want to know at the age of four or carrying the heavy burden of realizing that your mother doesn't love you. This pattern of her mother's behavior still exists today.

According to the unwritten parent guide society holds up for a gauge, her mother was a good parent. Lera had enough food to eat, a warm clean house to live in, nice clothes and both parents sacrificed to raise her. Compared to other children she was fortunate. It almost sounds like whining when comparing her childhood to present day news stories. Yet, her mother's behavior left hundreds of emotional scars that have left their marks.

It took years to understand the hurt and erosion that constant lying, and criticism does to a child, the behavior she knew as her mother's. Hurtful words hurdled at her for as long as she could remember. Not all abuse is physical, sometimes it's mental and emotional and with her mother, in varied amounts, it was all three. Well placed words of abuse and lies shot out to pierce a heart and ricochet through a soul, used with the same force and intent to cause harms as any battlefield bullet, the victory sweeter, the death slower, the assault neither physically traceable nor held accountable. Word bullets fired at close range with the skill of a practiced marksman.

The waiting was endless and so were Lera's thoughts. The surgery was finally over, and the family was informed that their mother had been moved to Critical Care. They walk together as a united group through the double doors towards the Recovery Room, past the noise of life-giving machines and the smell of sterile conditions. Their mother had been in surgery for nine hours. Doctors are all around her. She is lying unconscious in her hospital bed all swollen and blue. Tubes are coming out of her nose, mouth, stomach, chest and heart. IVs are going into mother's arms, legs and neck. Monitors are all around her clicking, beeping, issuing vital information.

The serious voice of the Surgeon pulls their attention around to him as he says, "Your mother is very, very critical. The surgery was more complicated than we had planned. After removing the sack from around her heart we also had to remove old the scar tissue from the previous three open-heart surgeries. Her heart had to be opened again due to blood clots. Your mother is on a machine to make her heart work and a respirator to help her breathe. It will take three days before we know if she will live or die. We'll be giving you more information in an hour."

The Family has all been in this place before. Family dysfunction was put aside as they pulled together to meet the crisis, and the routine kicked in. Schedules were arranged for someone to always be at the hospital during this critical time. It looks like Lera would be spending more hours at the hospital, one of the responsibilities of being the oldest.

Long, dark, nighttime hours in the waiting room cause her mind to drift back to her pain. The Inner voice says, "Face IT Lera." With a heavy sigh she finally has the courage to take a hard look at what is causing so much turmoil. Lera's body and mind shutter.... Oh God! Is that it, something so simple yet so real? Anger swells up bitterly in her throat and takes away her breath. Anger surges towards her mother for not loving her, for being the person who caused her hurt, instead of the person duty-bound to protect her. Sadness wells up in her very soul because her mother never bothered to find out how special Lera was. Anger burns white hot because her mother took all the wonderful things about her and turned them into something to be criticized or called defective.

Sadness at her brother waters her eyes. Once her best playmate, now someone who is willing believes all the lies their mother told him about her, without once questioning or asking Lera the truth. Anger, sadness, resentment, vulnerability press down hard. It is too much to process! It is difficult for her to breathe! Will she be held forever hostage by past hurts, shackled to the anger of family dysfunction?

Lera's body registers discomfort. Why is there a catch in her back and cramp in her left leg? Conscious thought works its way up through a black tunnel of sleep. Slowly her brain focuses on surroundings and her cramped position in the waiting room chair. Reality seeps into her tired eyes. How unusual to look over at complete strangers sleeping on waiting-room couches and chairs in assorted positions of disarray only a few feet away and in some distorted way it feels normal because we are all suffering from some form of crisis.

Sadness fills her chest. Regardless of the pain, her plight is nothing compared to the man on the next couch. He is in her age group and of all the dozens of families here Lera felt most drawn to him. She didn't know his name, only his story. Their eyes frequently connect and somehow an understanding and companionship of raw pain is shared. He is here because his wife, of a few months, broke her neck while they were riding on a four-wheeler with one of her children. The vehicle turned over while climbing a hill and, in an effort, to save her child she was injured. She will never walk again. Even though it was not his fault, and a child was saved, he feels responsible and the serious reality of their newly married future weighs heavy on his shoulders. Lera's situation, compared to his, is almost trivial. Her heart aches for him.

The pre-dawn update on her mom's first morning after surgery doesn't offer much change. The Critical Care schedule allows her to visit her unconscious mother fifteen minutes every hour. The respirator helped pull eight pounds of fluid from her mother's body that was pressing on her heart and lungs. The doctor informs Lera that another twenty-two pounds of fluid will need to be removed.

The routine of her long night merges into the day. Soon Lera will be able to visit her mother one last time before leaving for a break and bath, and the next shift of family members will be coming soon to take their turn. It will be so nice to leave the hospital for a while. A stiff, aching body registers the long drive from out-of-state and thirty hours since her pre-surgery arrival.

One of the hardest nights of her life was facing her past, present and future all at the same time, while waiting to see if her mother would live or die.

Circles hang dark under guarded eyes, but you can see a wounded glimmer if you look closely. There is tenderness in her heart from accepting the knowledge that her mother didn't love her with the same definition of love that she understood. Lera still tries to love her mother regardless of all the pain that she always inflicts.

Her mother has been an okay parent as much as she has been a bad one. Lera can justify her hurt feelings, but justification is a cold reward. Without the justification of being the victim she feels like she has nothing. Lera is so tired of hurting.

It felt so good for Lera's to be back in her own home and a whole state away from family. Six days of being with her family felt like a second lifetime. Her mother's planned release from the hospital, also released Lera. Finally, she is away from them, away from the hospital, away from all the tension of a mother's life-long illness that was never far away, and for most of Lera's life, has always been lying in wait to spring an appearance.

A two-month progress report, a second last-minute surgery was required on her mother's gallbladder before she could leave the hospital. Last week her brother had to take their mother back to the hospital for a couple of days because her blood was too thin. Regardless of all the recovery steps, her mother is doing well enough for someone who is seventy-one years old and has had four open-heart surgeries under her belt. Their mother continues to improve but will probably never have the quality of life or independence she was trying for, regardless of all she has endured to obtain it. She does have her life and hopefully that will be enough for her.

Old patterns and conditions that have always been part of Lera's relationship with her mother still exist. They survive because her mother doesn't choose to change them. The difference is that Lera no longer allows herself to be wounded by her mother's consistent and hurtful word bullets.

The relationship with her mother changed in a small way. Maybe because Lera has been driving a six-hour roundtrip every weekend to take care of her mother and relieve her brother. She has been doing this since the surgery in May, and it is now September. Lera still has trouble with the way her mother expresses love, if it is love. But her mother is her parent, and nothing can change that fact, nor would she want to. Their relationship may never be rewarding or loving but she is Lera's only living parent. It is a small price to pay for the person who gave you life and if you value your life then that is a debt worth paying.

That night in May taught Lera to love at a deeper, more unconditional level, and her mother may never get it... or her. The good news is that the self-induced surgery Lera did to open her own heart has now helped her to love herself and with that love comes forgiveness and understanding in the relationship she has with her mother.

Lera and her mother both had open-heart-surgery on that faith-filled-day in May and both are making the most of their repaired hearts... each in their own way.

Picket Fence

By L. J. Shook

The air of a late spring day felt cool against my skin as I sat on my parents' porch. Their house was in a nice neighborhood, on a quiet street that provided the perfect opportunity to listen to the birds gather in the trees and argue with the squirrels. I had made huge progress with my mother's flower beds, the yard and dad's aging picket fence. Six weeks of planting, fixing, trimming, mowing, and painting around my parents' house has given me a warm glow of satisfaction and brought a soft smile to my features, all the things that my father would be doing if he were able.

My thoughts seem to drift back to a happier time and a different fence. It was my first time painting and Grandma's fence was a wonderful time in my childhood when I stayed at her Illinois home. My Father's Mother lived in the country and had the best things a young child could want. There was a big wood to explore, water that needed to be pumped and lots of hills to roll down. She had chickens that wanted to be fed, eggs to gather, a huge garden to hoe, and wonderful meals with fresh vegetables and homemade pies. Dinners and lunches were made with vegetables I help harvest, apples that I picked went into Grandma's pies that she let me roll out and cut.

My favorite place was an old barn where I could spend endless hours exploring and a rope swing tied to a large oak tree that flew out over a shallow creek filled with toads and crawdads. What made the biggest impression was the fence that Grandmother let me paint. I pretended to be a great painter like my dad and granny. The fence was my canvas.

Grandma's fence was the beginning of my life. My parents' fence represents an ending, the ending of a valuable life. Dad's fence has served as my release. It has been an outlet for my anger and frustration, a place to find a reprieve from my father's dying, and my opportunity to think. It was my place to cry, away from the eyes and ears of my parents.

Life can take many sharp turns in such a short period of time. In the span of a few weeks, I went from a working divorced mother with my own apartment to an unemployed daughter that spends part of each day scraping and painting an old picket fence. This is a story of beginnings, endings and choices.

It was my choice to put my furniture in storage and move in with my parents. The decision was made with sadness, regret and love. Dad is two years into his late-stage cancer, and it has only been a couple years since my mother's second open-heart surgery.

Dad was always my anchor in the storm, my teacher of art and life, the parent that loved and liked me. He protected me and helped me to understand humor, honor and the joy of telling a story. Dad was the first man I loved. How could I let the painful passing of my father go without slowing down my life to notice?

So many people conduct life like they are in a fast car on a four-lane highway and a death or illness in the family equals a 10-minute rest stop along their interstate of living. I couldn't let my father go without taking notice... without letting dad know I wanted and needed to capture every second we had left together.

When I moved in with my parents, I thought it would be a short-term stay, a month at the most. I had underestimated my father's will to live. It was still my choice to continue to the end. A choice made not with courage or wisdom but with sacrifice and love.

My many months of adjustment were hard, from mother back to daughter, from independent to dependent, from woman with a future to child of the past. Weeks and months spent nursing, feeding and bathing dad. My puttering, mowing and painting around their old house was just a way to escape from the reality of my father's future. When the anxiety of watching my dad die slowly and painfully overwhelmed me, or the strain of being inactive bothered me I would work on Dad's picket fence.

The need for my beloved Father to get well and live forever did battle with my need to get on with my life and my own family. When the pressure became too much I worked on dad's time-worn fence. It served me well that fence of tears.

Dad had such a beautiful heart. I watched family and friends drift in and out of the house daily to support and love my father. What a wonderful tribute for a life well lived. Of all the choices I have made in my life this was the very hardest and the best. I was able to give dad his wish to die at home. But the greatest gift of all was mine. I was given the opportunity and time to show dad how much I loved and appreciated him as a parent and a person.

How many times in life do we get the chance to express our feelings fully, at the time it is needed and wanted the most? The pain of being a caregiver for my father while he was dying was so strong at times that I could barely breathe. But if I had avoided the hurt of loving and helping my father while he died, then I would have missed all the special moments, and the memories shared those last precious months. Sometimes the things that we grieve the most are the opportunities lost, or those special moments that change our lives forever, but their importance went unrecognized until it was too late to express our gratitude.

If I have learned nothing else, it is this... the only day we have is today. The past is gone, and the future is only a promise, not a guarantee. It is better to not grieve regrets but gather memories. Seize the now and love it with all your heart.

Radio Man

By L. J. Shook

This past weekend I rented a movie, the title was, "Radio." Like so many things in life, the timing of the movie at the theater slipped by before I got my act together. So, I did like everyone else and waited until it came out on video.

I rented the movie and settled down for an evening at the movies, home-style. The movie's plot was centered on a character played by Cuba Gooding Jr., whose nickname was, "Radio." The movie lived up to all my expectations, but the whole time I watched it I thought of the local man that we have been calling, "Radio Man," long before the movie came out. Our, "Radio Man," whose real name is Tim, isn't black or handicapped except for the multiple personalities that he displays when purchasing gas or buying a soda. The reason we called our home-grown character, "Radio Man," was because he made static noises before he talked that sounded like the static on a radio. It was like his several personalities kept him tuned into multiple frequencies all the same time.

There was just something that appealed to me about our Radio Man and I went out of my way to be nice to him. Radio Man once thought he was treated badly by one of the cashiers, so he went home and called back at work to tell her she was fired. One time when giving Tim his change he told me, "I've got to stop buying this Vanilla Coke because Jeff says it's killing him." Jeff was one of Tim's other personalities.

No one wanted to wait on Radio Man because he had wild, greasy hair, with a dirty ball cap that sat sideways on his head. His fingernails were long and dirty and his clothes unwashed and ragged. His pants were two sizes too big, and he didn't' have a belt. He was constantly holding his pants in front to keep them in place and the thought of his pants falling was a constant worry for him and me. His hands were generally dirty from lack of water or soap and sometimes he smelled so bad that you had to take a deep breath before getting close enough to take his money for his purchase. It was a rite of passage for a new cashier to look up and be deserted by all the other cashiers so she would have to wait on Radio Man alone. We didn't want the new person to miss out on the experience of our Radio Man.

I didn't mind waiting on him, except for the summer days when the smell was a lot stronger. There was something kind and searching in his eyes that drew my attention and I would go out of my way to speak to Tim and inquire into how he was doing. Sometimes it was Tim that answered and sometimes it was Jeff, or maybe someone else whose name I didn't know, but he was always Radio Man with that static noise he made before he answered. Some of the most outrageous things would come out of his mouth, and I would smile and laugh, not because I was making fun of him but because he was, "one of a kind."

Part of me envied his ability to be so disconnected and unconcerned about what was going on in the world around him. I have wished several times, when my kids were teenagers, that I could escape reality for just a little while. I'm not saying I want to be mentally ill or have multiple personalities. But sometimes, occasionally, it would have been nice to escape some of the hard drama of teens.

Radio Man didn't show up for his vanilla coke for few months and people at the store commented that they hadn't seen him. Then one day I was waiting on a customer and Radio Man's voice spoke to me, but the person didn't look anything like Radio Man. I took a second glance, and standing before me was a clean-shaven, well manicured, nicely dressed, young man. His hair was clean and cut, he was wearing glasses, and his clothes were new. My astonishment showed on my face and in my voice when I asked him, "Tim, what have you done to yourself? You look good." His answer was, "I was getting bad, wasn't I?"

Tim is now in a Group Home, taking medication, well fed, and looked after. Jeff is gone as well as the other personalities and Tim will no longer need to be concerned about drinking those awful Vanilla Cokes and upsetting Jeff.

I'm sincerely happy for Tim that he is no longer neglected. This truly is an answer to one of my prayers for him, but part of me misses Radio Man. I wouldn't want Tim to ever go hungry and neglected again, but there was something special about our Radio Man, like the character in my movie.

Maybe it is just the loss of an original character. In life so many people are trying to imitate movie stars and sport athletes, or people they think are important in the world. Originals seem to be in short supply, these days, and our Radio Man was one of my original experiences.

Raindrops Keep Falling on Your Head

By L. J. Shook

You know my kids tell me in a kind, but not so complimentary way, that I have this way of dripping on them until I get their attention or open their eyes enough to consider another avenue or point of view. To date, that has been one of their best compliments given to me, even though it wasn't meant as a compliment at the time.

I have always had this fascination with raindrops, the way a drop of water hits the ground and causes ripples in the puddles of raindrops that came before it. Hours have been spent watching one raindrop cause a ripple that goes out and touches another ripple and another. This is how I think wisdom and love move through life, by one wave or ripple touching another wave or ripple and another. Everyone who is standing close or in range of the ripple of wisdom and love is engulfed and affected like radio waves that are received and heard but never seen.

Rain can be gentle and nurturing, serious and threatening, or forceful and destructive. When a raindrop joins other raindrops it becomes rain and when rain joins with wind all sorts of things can happen.

My goal has never been to be a hurricane or driving force in my children's lives but rather a gentle reminder, like a raindrop, of how great their spirits are. Rocks have been altered, rivers formed, grand canyons craved out, and a rain forest nurtured by one raindrop at a time. I have never underestimated my strength in being a constant drip on my children. My dripping hasn't always gotten the effect I wanted but just knowing that if I couldn't get their attention being a persistent irritation was enough for me, like a nice rewarding side effect.

This week, for the very first time, I was given a glimpse of how all three of my children are growing into their adulthood in a wonderful and rewarding way. I must tell you there have been times that I thought I was just watering a rock. At odd times through the years, I have seen moments of maturity and possibility flash before me, but those were random, fleeting and never as a whole group. But this week I was given a look at the fruit that was produced from all those love drops that I have dripped over them in the past forty years.

Just knowing that I had created a ripple that has touched my children's ripple, and their ripples are touching my grandchildren's ripples was one of those, "WOW," moments for a mother. Our conversations this week were about memories of my father and how his ripples in our lives had caused us all to be better people, better children and better grandchildren.

I have been thinking about how important water is becoming in our struggling world and the power of those raindrops are needed even more than ever before. My father's love drips are still being felt twenty years after his passing. So, I hope my children know that alive or dead I will be that persistent raindrop dripping on their heads for years and years to come.

Rough Diamond

By L. J. Shook

Soulful eyes watch me, mysterious and deep
signaling a secret, a truth, a promise that sleeps.

Something tugs at me and draws me to your side,
a hidden force sweeps me up on an emotional tide.

Stirred and attracted beyond my will,
My heart skips a beat, my mind won't still.

Eyes drawn to yours and can't look away,
Destiny calls and asks me to stay.

Where have you been... I've waited so long,
yearning for the music of your heart's song?

Your spark has magic... my diamond in the rough,
sweet, vulnerable, manly and so tenderly tough.

You are of immeasurable value, unrecognized worth.
An unearthed treasure... recovered spirit given birth.

The heat of your flame draws close to mine.
Passion sparks and our essences entwine.

You get me... like no other man
Soul-filled touches, like no one else can.

You pull into your lungs the passion of my breath
Vibrations sear along my spine and give love a test.

The touch of your spirit and imprint of your hand
claims my heart and leaves a mark like a brand.

Run, Me Maw, Run

By L. J. Shook

I have heard it said a thousand times that being a grandparent is great but couldn't fully understand this phenomenon until I became one myself. No one had explained to me about the catch I would get in my throat, or the stalled breathing, the swelling of love in my heart to the point of pain when seeing the child of my child. I was not prepared for the instant and fierce bond or the overwhelming level of love that infiltrated into every cell of my being. Your own children impact your heart and your life, and you think that is all there is until you have a grandchild, and then you realize there is a whole new level of unconditional love you didn't know existed.

I don't know if these feelings happen through maturity, wisdom, or the freedom of not having the full burden of parental responsibility weighing so heavily on your shoulders. When being a parent, the pressure, "To Get it right," is almost crippling. I was determined to do a better job of parenting than my own parents. The knowledge of how screwed up a parent can make a child is in the news, the movies, at school, in the eyes of the people around you when your child throws a fit in public, or in the way we view our own personal lives. After all, I know that I could have won the Nobel Peace Prize by now if it hadn't been for the way my mother parented me.

I recently went to my two-year-old grandson's birthday party. For this event I drove two hundred miles and willingly spent time in the group presence of my ex-husband, his new wife and my ex-Mother-In-Law. This was an occurrence that bribery, gunpoint, or torture would not have forced me into doing under any other circumstances. Since I would walk on hot coals for my grandchildren what's the big deal in handling an old ex-husband and his new wife.

The next day I took a vacation day from my job so I could spend the whole time with my grandson while his parents went to work. Imagine, a full day of fun, with a brand new two-year-old. My daughter's worried looks on whether old mom could handle such a busy little boy were her concerns, but not mine. Dylan and I both wanted to do the same things, play in the park, go low on the slide, high in the swing and investigate everything in between. We were on an adventure and partners in the discovery of life.

Between the park and naptime, we took Happy Meals back to my daughter's house. Dylan has a great level of communication, even though most sentences are only two or three words long. He had no problem in making his wishes known.

This is where the perks of being a grandparent come into play, because I didn't have to say, "NO," once during our day together. It wasn't the fact that Dylan didn't try to misbehave, or that I am such a lenient grandparent that I didn't make him follow the rules. The truth is that my daughter and son-in-law have already taught Dylan the rules, and all the, "NO s," in his house. He probably has heard, "NO," more times than he has days in his young life. I know he has spent more time standing in the corner than most little boys his age, except for maybe, his Uncle Jason. I have wondered at times, if Dylan's forehead would be the shape of a triangle by the time he is ten from all the standing-in-corner time he has already logged.

When Dylan tried to smear catsup on the table at lunch all I had to do was ask him a question, "Does Mom let you make a mess, Dylan?" He looked up at me with a grownup stare and answered, "Nooo." I then quietly asked him, "Well, why are you doing it?" He stopped making a mess and looked at me again with the most honest, bad-boy smile and a dimple appeared on his left cheek. My smile broadened Dylan's smile and we both laughed. I have seen that same smile a million times before over the last twenty-six years...from his mother.

Dylan wasn't trying to be bad, nor did he need to relearn the rules. He was just making sure the boundaries were still in place with the new boss in town.

That day with my two-year-old grandson was one of my happiest. The memories of those snuggles at naptime, the gift of reading a story to a captive audience, the freedom he gave me to run and play, hide and seek, to again make mounds and castles in the sand are with me even today. But his greatest birthday gift to me was hearing his squeals of pure joy in being chased around the picnic table. His words still ring in my heart, "Run, Me Maw, Run."

I have those words posted on my computer and several times a day I read them and remember that even though I feel old I am still young, carefree and the whole world is still out there for me to discover. The gift of life is, this moment, pure joy and love can be as simple to find as running free with my grandson around the picnic table on a warm day.

Rylee, Happy First 2013

By Grammy Shook

She entered this world during a
storm...on the tail of a big wind.

Her arrival caused ripples
and put the family in a spin.

Her grunts and coos soon turned
into smiles and charmed every heart.

She is funny and smart; nothing about her
has been ordinary... even from the start.

She has a smile like an angel,
that will brighten your day.

And the charm of a gambler,
that lingers and stays.

She is the product of teasers, four generations strong,
She doesn't like to be told no, or that she is wrong.

With hugs, and loves she can make your day
then tease with kisses she won't give away.

She is part karma from her parents' past deeds
and gene pool product of a family's wacky seeds.

I pray Rylee, that your life's path be guided from above.
And you will always know support from your family's love.

Santa's Letter for Martha

Dear Martha,

My Naughty Girl Radar has been bleeping and your name has flashed on the screen a few times. It is a good thing you aren't naughty all the time, only once in a while, because that would be more serious.

I noticed that you turned a hundred years old this year. It is hard to believe that I have been bringing you presents for a century. The time does fly.

One of the Elves told me that you were being too frisky in the yard and fell and broke your wrist. I'm glad that you are doing better.

Try and keep your frisky behavior down. I will look forward to seeing you again this year for the hundredth time. No coal or switches this year only good cheer.

Have a Merry Christmas.

Santa and Rudolf

Settled In and Unsettled

By L. J. Shook

Settled, yes that's a good description. Settled in is how I have felt the last few years. Not over joyous but settled down and maintaining a steady keel after so many years of riding the turbulent seas of life. I'm comfortable working, writing, and painting pictures. I'm content to be more of an observer than a front-line participant. My dues are all paid up in the life-wars section and I am looking forward to my much-earned reprieve.

Grandchildren and friends take up most of my spare time, without the encumbrance of a husband or boyfriend to hold me back, weigh me down, or sensor my activities. Eighteen years of having a husband was enough for me. Thirty years of being single have suited me just fine. I revel in my singleness; embrace it with all my being. I enjoy it so much that it makes my family and friends uncomfortable.

Thoughts and ideas flow back and forth with an old friend on how we expect to spend the rest of our advancing years. My friend still wants to have that one good man in her life before she dies, someone to cancel out the memories of her two bad ex-husbands, but her plans are not mine.

I have stated, for years, the reason I don't date anymore is because I am waiting for the man strong enough to take me on, and then laugh because of the obvious contradiction in words to my true feelings. My friend and I agree our remaining years will not be spent playing bingo, sitting on a bench counting passing cars, or walking a little yappy dog. We both are very adamant about ailments and past surgeries, not being the only topic of conversation we are capable of having is our highlights and pros and cons of old-age medications.

I have always threatened my kids with the possibility of

buying a fast red scooter when serious old age starts rattling its chain, or at the very least doing something unpredictable and beyond the ordinary for someone in obvious impending years of decline. My children give me that leery-look bracing for what will come next, with expectations that I will start acting out my rebellion of getting older any day now. Just the thought that I can still scare them is satisfying enough... for now.

There hasn't even been a thought of a man in my life for several years. I am too busy in my pursuit of personal growth, being a Reiki Master, and expressing my creativity, to be slowed down. No manly dalliance of distraction for this chick.

I am always amazed at God's sense of humor and the unexpectedness of life showing up when I least expect it. So, you can imagine my discomfort and dismay when a tall, handsome, dark-haired, smooth-talking, younger man turned my head and I didn't look away, like I have done so many times before.

I thought about running, but his depth... his words surprised me, like a deer caught in a headlight, his stare singled me out. His eyes blazed with an intense spark of possibilities that I had long forgotten. This was a man, not just the ordinary full-grown male/child that currently permeates our society. The rarity of such a special species in my life was too unusual for me to not take notice and with just one look my interest was held captive. This was that one man strong enough to take me on.

It was my choice in whether to take up the challenge, after years of blustering about the strong man I had, for so long, claimed I required. My spirit vibrated with his rightness and strength, his arms of protectiveness, and take-charge manner, drew me like a moth to his flame. In all my life I don't think I have ever had a man that understood and has gotten me the way he does. I have been opening my own doors, carrying my own groceries, and changing my own flat tires for a very long time.

This man eased past my resolutions and changed a harden mind with one piercing stare. Who would have thought? How does a determined woman focused on a planned future get side-tracked? Why now... this game of attraction could have been played with any of the willing males that have extended offers over the last several years, the volunteers frequent and plentiful?

Past the age of fifty most people have already lived a lot, experienced most, and imagined the rest. By the age of sixty the drive to gather new experiences takes a back seat and in place of quantity we strive for quality, preferring truth over fantasy or illusion. There is a need for tranquility in mature life rather than high drama. Life's attraction is to search for meaning, rather than just piling up boastful events.

A person my age doesn't want to build a new house or expand a career. It is time to escape from the burden of being an indentured servant to the house and expected social behavior. The drive to make big career moves no longer holds any appeal and the idea of free time, and grandchildren have started to blossom in my mind. Let the young and eager chase the brass ring because I have already run my marathons.

Romance, at this age, takes on a whole different nuisance than in the past and there is a need to redefine what pairing with another really means. There are no thoughts of new family members, nor am I desperate for, "the one great love of my life." I have already encountered a wondrous love, and the memories of that experience are better than any reality of the men that I have dated since. So, I have settled in and comfortable with my singular existence, thinking that I have already had my allotment of romance and love, and I can now live out the rest of my life with gratitude for the memories and adventures of my younger years.

The unexpectedness of this man is what took me off guard. He didn't come to me in an overwhelming rush of passion or a lighting bolt of attraction but rather he was like the sea, powerful, deep, unpredictable... sending out waves that lapped at my feet inviting me to wade in and experience more. He felt like the beauty of a sunset that transforms a day, was I willing to look away in case he slipped below the horizon? Would I take up the challenge of the sea or run back to where my life is familiar and safe?

The sea beckoned and I waded in and swam in the deep blue of his soul. No one knows what the next day will bring. The past is like dust on the ground and the future is only a promise, like a sunrise.

Because of age we're not the heated pepper sprouts of our youth but rather blank pages of a budding novel, or the harmonious notes of a song being written. We blended together to become the new steps of an original dance. So far... I still want to read the next page, sing the next note, and dance the new steps. It is this reminder of who I once was and who I can become again with this sweet-talking man that holds my interest, regardless of all my past resolutions.

Our joining has been a rich, mellow symphony; a reflection of our maturity rather than a rush for gratification. Each kiss is like a note played by master musicians, the melody sweet, the tempo slowly deliberate, and the music more beautiful and breathtaking than the notes that came before. All I really have is NOW, this minute. So, for today... this day... I'm embracing the unknown and sailing in uncharted waters.

Regrets are for those that monitor their day by aches, pains, a houseful of cats and a full pill box. I would rather cry like a banshee, because I have loved and lost than forever wonder what I've missed. With grey hair caressing my temples, who would have thought there could be more fun living yet to be done by a person whose favorite name to be called is... "Grammy"?

Seventy and Six

By L. J. Shook

I always knew this day would come but was not sure when it would happen. In all honesty I was hoping that it would be a little farther down the road, but then at seventy, I learned to take things as they come without letting too many ripples rock my boat.

This last visit from my six-year-old granddaughter was my day of reckoning. A week earlier I had asked my forty-five-year-old daughter what she wanted for her birthday. After a couple days of thought she sent me a text saying she wanted a German chocolate cake and a break from her highly imaginative daughter for the whole weekend.

Hurray... Rylee and I have been comrades from the very beginning, from when I first saw her being born to that blessed day when she came to me every day as a baby to be watched over while her parents were at work. From the very first moment I held her, and she snuggled the best and wiggled her tiny head under my chin, I knew it was a match made in heaven.

At age three years Rylee needed more than I could give her physically and mentally, so her parents put her into preschool. She was starting to read words, and we all knew that we would have trouble keeping up with her active mind. Rylee is cute and has enough charm and intelligence to wrap her older brothers around her little finger. On Rylee's last visit she informed me it was just plain sad that I didn't have any electronic games on my smart phone.

It has been a bad winter, so I now have a mouse that has taken up residence. Like most grandmas my age I'm not fond of mice. They give me the ecks. I don't like killing anything, so I didn't really want to kill the little bugger. I just wanted him to live somewhere else. I started off by getting a glue box trap with plans on just throwing him outside once he got stuck and he could chew his way out... outside. But the mouse chewed into the back of the box and got the peanut butter without ever going into the glue part. This mouse is starting to get on my nerves, and the urge to do him bodily harm is getting stronger. So, I decided that it was time to bring in the big guns and I bought an old-fashioned mouse trap. He cleaned it off without tripping it. I have tried old wooden mouse traps, newfangled mouse traps and all sorts of mouse traps in between. I just want him to go! He has forced me to buy the dreaded mouse poison with pictures of dead mice on the cover, but I am having trouble deciding to put it out. Someone told me that mice don't like the smell of Irish Spring soap, so in a last-ditch effort I have left pieces of soap everywhere but now I am finding his little teeth marks on the Irish Spring. The plan of getting this mouse has become a personal issue for me with thoughts of his demise.

A couple of days before my granddaughter's planned weekend visit, she was tested in kindergarten, and they are placing her in accelerated classes when she goes into first grade. She was already reading before she went to preschool. So now I am going to spend my weekend with a smart granddaughter and a smart mouse at the same time. That's a lot to ask of a seventy-year-old grandmother. I tried talking her parents into bringing her cat, Gracie, for a visit at the same time but when they all arrived there was no cat, only a caravan of three suitcases, and several bags of fuzzy blankets, snacks, dolls, stuffed animals and any other items Rylee couldn't live without. After three trips to load their van, they drew the line on bringing a live cat, litter and food. It was more than they wanted to deal with.

First thing Rylee informs me she doesn't want me to kill my mouse she wants me to catch it and gently put it outside. You have got to be kidding. I do not touch mice. I have spent seventy years not touching a mouse and I am not going to start now. I don't even remove mice from the trap, I use long handled barbecue tongs and throw the trap and mouse both out the door.

My granddaughter has decided that my mouse must be hungry, because after meals I clean up all the crumbs and put the bread or anything that might be food for an over smart mouse in the refrigerator so he can't get to it. Unless the mouse has already learned how to open the frig door by now. After I cleaned up my granddaughter very quietly, and secretly started leaving little pieces of food and snacks everywhere, so the little mouse wouldn't starve.

I had suggested to her that if he was hungry, he might decide to go live somewhere else, but to no avail. If I could figure how to do it, I would put that obnoxious mouse in her suitcase and send him home with her... where she and Gracie the cat both live.

I tried to distract her by saying if we collected all the snacks and food that she didn't eat we could feed the homeless cat that I see in the neighborhood. I thought this would satisfy her need to love all animals without causing me to have a 500-pound mouse in my house. The plan was for her to take three steps, put the plate on the front porch and then bring in her booster seat from the outside chair where it had been left and forgotten. Rylee put on her shoes but not her coat, at best this plan would take five seconds in my thoughts but not hers. She carries the plate of food out the door like a ceremonial offering but instead of putting the plate on the porch she goes down the steps and wades through the snow to take it to the driveway so the cat can't miss it. On her way back I reminded her to grab the booster seat which is what tipped the scales.

Those two extra steps set her off. She stomps inside with the booster seat, like only an indignant six-year-old can, and informs me she is cold, and it is my fault, because I wouldn't let her wear her coat!

Really! Instead of stating the obvious that she refused to wear her coat, I took a deep breath and gave her THE look. Then

I quietly said, "I'm probably a terrible grandma...I think you should fire me!" She loudly informs me, "I can't."

It was not a, "I love you too much I could never fire you grandma," sort of statement. It was more of a, "We are related, and I'm stuck with you," sort of declaration. My day of reckoning was here, at the age of my seventy and her six.

Later, after several games and stories along with hugs and kisses it was time to take Rylee, her three suitcases, and the several bags of dolls, blankets and numerous things she just couldn't live without back home. But without the mouse. The night before I slipped a cracker in her open suitcase hoping the mouse would crawl in and go home with her, but that plan backfired. I think the mouse was gorged and sleeping off his food coma from the trail of snacks secretly left for him.

Now that I was back in my sanctuary, I had to face the chore of dealing with my now obese mouse. Putting the poison around for the mouse still made me feel icky but Mr. Mouse had overstayed his welcome. Thank goodness he didn't die in the wall but behind the furniture and all I had to do was sweep him into the dustpan and throw his squishy body outside... gagging all the way.

I guess we are all capable of murder if pushed far enough. I am now a premeditated murderer at seventy, sick about it... but not remorseful.

Showdown at Register Three

By L. J. Shook

The drive had been long and boring and with his free hand he scratches his unruly and unkempt whiskers. Bright lights from his favorite fuel stop appear on the horizon. Hopefully that redhead will be working tonight. Something about her bothers him and gets under his skin, forcing him to give her a rough time. With any luck he will be able to get her mad and bring out her feisty nature. He likes the way her green eyes sparkle when he gets her temper up.

Just one more night of work and it will be her day off, Thank God! The weather has been frigid and snowy which has caused the drivers to be cranky and rude. Her patience is frazzled and she's not sure how much longer she can reframe herself from doing bodily harm to one of them.

Nash, the other cashier, removes the aluminum tire thumper that someone left on the counter next to her register; in fear she might start using it to thump the bad customers. Redheads are unpredictable with a low flash point. He didn't want to take any chances that it might be a rude truck driver's unlucky night.

The door opens and cold air blows through the fuel desk. Nash gives a shiver and an inward sigh. NOT THAT GUY AGAIN. He was the one that riled her up last night. This was not a good night for Whiskers and the Redhead to be in proximity to each other.

Whiskers wander the isles of the store, finding his items and then makes a beeline to the Redhead's register even though she has a line of customers and Nash's register is open.

She grits her teeth in anticipation as Whiskers sets his purchases on her counter. He has had the same set of clothes on for the whole week and each day new food droppings are added to the front of his shirt. He is retired and now working as a bank courier. His behavior and tired jokes mark him as an old trucker as much as his worn plaid shirts. The Redhead rings up his pile of junk food and makes the mistake of asking him if he would like a bag for his items. Whiskers replies, "No thanks I left my ole bag at home. Ha. Ha."

The redhead ignores him. It is one of the stupidest comments that truckers make, and she had heard it a million times before. She didn't like the comment the first time she heard it, let alone a million times later. You would think that with all the time they have been driving up and down the road they would eventually be able to come up with some new lines instead of just repeating the same worn-out old ones all the time.

When Whiskers doesn't get the reaction he wants, he asks the Redhead if she has heard him. She ignores him again in hopes he will let it drop and continue out the door.

Whiskers caught her bristle when he repeated his comment. So, he adds, "Oh never mind, I already divorced that old bag," then laughs at his own joke, as if he had voiced some rare pearl of humor.

Nash had to grin despite himself. Like two gunslingers at Okay Corral, they take their positions and make their stand... the Redhead and Whiskers.

Nash knew the Redhead was having family problems and had been struggling with maintaining her cool... no doubt about it, Whiskers had just stepped over the line into the danger zone. He was glad he had removed the tire thumper from her register. He would have felt sorry for the old guy if he hadn't known that Whiskers was purposely doing it to irate her and really did deserve all that was going to come his way.

The Redhead replies, "No wonder your wife divorced you. Any woman would divorce you too if you referred to her as an old bag."

Whiskers fires his second shot. "I'll never get married again!"

The Redhead fires back, "You couldn't give me all the money there is to get married again!"

Whiskers puff out his chest like he has bragging rights, loads up and fires again. "I've been divorced since 1993."

The Redhead is quick on the draw and returns fire, "Well I've been divorced since, "86.""

• Whiskers fires off another round, "My wife got remarried two months after our divorce." The smoke from his last shot waffled through the air.

He has her now.

The Redhead smiles like a cat with cream on its tongue and quietly replies "My ex-husband was married two weeks after my divorce."

Whiskers, steps back, aims and then fires his last shot, "Why buy the cow when the milk is free?" Smoke, from this tried-and-true poison dart circles his plaid shirt.

His last comment has never failed him yet. It is guaranteed to irritate any self-respecting woman, Whiskers waits, and the silence causes him to grin. He finally has her now!!!!

The air crackles with tension and her green eyes flash with sparks. With a deceptive calm voice, the red-haired word-slinger aims dead center and fires, "Why...buy...a...bull...when...the...only...thing..you...get...is...BULL POOP!!"

The smoke clears and Whiskers' ammunition is all used up, and he is not smart enough to think up his own word bullets, so he gathers his bag of supplies and walks towards the exit. Before pushing through the door, he stops and gives the Redhead a broad smile and wink, "Be good. I'll see you again tomorrow night."

The unimpressed redhead rolls her eyes and mumbles, "Old Dog."

Nash laughs out loud and shakes his head. Another old trucker on a fool's errand has just registered on the, "Stupid Man

Don't Know When to Stop Meter." If he were a betting man, he would have to put his money on the Redhead. He has worked with her long enough to know her rapid-fire-wit has beaten the best of them, and there doesn't seem to be a shortage of men on a fool's errands for her to practice on.

Small and Simple Challenges

By L J Shook

Plunk...plunk, two hard thrusts on the pump forces just the right amount of lotion into my hand. A wet, smooth, crackle emanates from the space between my palms. One hand rub hard against the other to transfer my body heat into the cool, thick cream as a pleasant, medicine smell whiffs up to tickle my nose. Friction quickly warms the lotion, and I move closer to the hospital bed. My hands move slowly over spasmodic legs trying to rub out the jerking and protesting muscle as they are trying to be straightened. Light flickers off rows of trophies and medals, displayed on shelves in the next room.

Every night is the same; remove Harrison's upper clothes, transfer his catheter bag, comb his hair, brush his teeth and wash a handsome face. Large hooks, attached to chains on a Hoyer Lift and slip into metal on his cloth seat.

Pump, pump, the action reminds me of pumping water at my grandmother's old farmhouse when I was a child. This action drives a hydraulic piston that lifts Harrison up from his wheelchair.

Momentarily his body swings free.

Harrison's nightly moment of freedom from his invisible jailer is also the most vulnerable part of his day, memories involving bruised ribs, bumps, bangs and a variety of rough treatment inflicted by the large turnover of under skilled caregivers, cross his mind. His moment of freedom is always overshadowed by past experiences.

Amid our nightly debates about the woman's place, politics, love, religion, and the evening news, Harrison's body hovers over his air bed as I take off his shoes, trying to untie his double knotted shoelaces tied by his morning caregiver. We both chuckle at the absurdity of this precaution. Harrison's broken thirty-four-year-old body is unable to move his legs in his wheelchair or in any way trip over shoelaces that might come untied.

His broken back, fifth vertebra down, doesn't give his paralyzed body the luxury of tying his own shoes, washing his face, dressing or undressing and the several hundred other things that we all take so blatantly for granted every day.

With his shoes and socks removed, the turn of one knob slowly lowers Harrison onto his hospital bed. Now a body bent from sitting for twelve or more hours must try and adjust to lying flat. Rolling Harrison to his right and then left side allows me to remove the Hoyer Lift seat and the rest of his clothing. A young man, World-Class athlete, lies broken before me. During a national competition, in his quest to gain Olympic status in Kick Boxing, a match went bad and brought down this mighty oak.

I readjust my hands and brace my body to absorb his uncontrollable spasms that threaten to knock him out of bed, his muscles bump hard against my efforts to calm his out-of-control body. I apply lotion to dark brown skin, trying to massage and smooth out hard tense muscles. The cool lotion is a nightly ritual, skin breakdown and bed sores are as serious a concern for Harrison as catching a cold would be because of his limited breathing ability.

Harrison's body continues to have spasms but lessen as my actions smooth his legs straight again. He is grateful for the temporary spasms because they give his body exercise and help to keep his muscles toned. Being paralyzed, for Harrison, means that he can't feel his legs or control the movement, but his muscles still work. If I don't get his final alignment just right; the position that Harrison must lay in for the rest of the night, then he will have hard and severe cramps in his legs and back all night, which do bring discomfort and being paralyzed takes away his ability to straighten or move in any way to correct the hard knotted muscles in his body.

I once asked Harrison how he handles, "It," every day? Harrison confessed to me tonight that his brothers had come over for a visit and had gotten into an argument with each other and because he was unable to push his own wheelchair, he couldn't even leave the room.

He confided to me how cocky and self-assured he was as a younger man, questing for fame and riches while expressing a loud critical opinion of under-achievers. Always taking it for granted he would have good health and unlimited strength. In Harrison's dreams he longs for his past, when he had a girlfriend, trained for his sport, traveled the country, and took one thought-free step after another.

Today Harrison's wheelchair-bond-body struggles to lift his arms and maneuver paralyzed hands. This highly trained athlete and world traveler prays for the opportunity to function on a level he would have once scoffed at.

A urinal replaces his condom catheter. Pillows are placed around his body and between his ankles to prevent bed sores. A muscular but broken body is covered with a sheet and blanket as I tucked him in for the night. My nightly duties are complete. Before I leave, my last act of service is to give Harrison a cool drink of water and flip the pillow under his head, to the cool side. He said that I was the only one who had ever thought to do that for him. Green eyes, look into his brown eyes, and our final smile is shared. Putting Harrison to bed only takes an hour out of my night... somehow it feels like more.

It's 12:30 am, crisp air meets me as Harrison's front door closes behind me. Breathing freely becomes a newfound luxury, and I savor each deep breath.

It takes two jobs for a single woman my age to survive in this struggling economy and I lost my full-time, "pay-the-rent-job," today. The State Revenue Department sent me a letter yesterday saying I owe a year's worth of taxes because my ex-employer deceived me when he said taxes were taken out of my paycheck.

There are no savings and little money in my bank account. Rosie, the bomb, overheated this morning from a hole in the radiator and my left front tire continues to have a slow persistent leak.

As I walk to my car I skip to the middle of the dark, deserted street, turn my face upward to look at the stars and whisper a quiet prayer of thanks. Harrison has shown me, what I thought were overwhelming problems just an hour ago, are nothing more than temporary inconveniences.

"Thank You God... for my small and simple challenges."

Sometimes You Get It Right

By L. J. Shook

There are many experiences that bring back memories of a dumb decision or bad mistake that have made a mark on my life with indelible ink. I can still recall those flashes of humility that are craved deep in my memory, where they hover and stand ready to remind me of my frequent stupidity.

But once, I got it right and surprised myself and the people around me by grasping that golden moment and doing it right. For me, that moment in time was during my father's last months. I didn't know much about getting through this journey of life, but I did know that I loved my father. My father's cancer devastated me but what I did about it freed my soul. It wasn't so much that I grabbed the moment but more like the moment grabbed me and didn't let go.

The thing that drove me like a sheep herder was the thought I didn't want my father to pass away and leave this world without knowing for sure how much I loved him and the great example of being a parent he set. So many times, we leave words unsaid that later become our regret. I didn't want to have any regrets, or dad to have any doubt about how I felt.

My father told humorous stories about people he knew. He wasn't a writer and didn't write his stories down, he just told them. And my father was a painter. Every person and every canvas were a story being told.

Mostly my father painted stories on canvas of horses in wild western scenes with shades of brown landscapes and blues skies. I'm not sure if the pictures came from Zane Grey books, he read or a secret dream to be a cowboy. It doesn't matter; his fun-loving personality and creative flare were all part of the wealth of my father's life.

When dad's body became so sick he could no longer get out of bed I moved back home to help my mother nurse him. I still remember the day that I made the decision. It was a cold, miserable, winter day that started with me looking for a new apartment.

My life had reached a crossroad, and I was ready for a change. I found a great apartment, but something held me back from signing the lease. I told the owner that I needed to think about it and would let him know the next day. I went home and covered up at the corner of my couch to contemplate my future. My head nodded and woke me up from my dream. There had been a person in my dream that had asked me a question. Did I want to move upward or forward? I thought that was such a strange question. In the dream I chose to move upward and there was no looking back after that moment. Moving forward was to sign the lease for the new apartment but moving upward was to move back home and take care of my father.

It has been my observation that moving upward, in a spiritual way, doesn't always feel like upward and sometimes to go upward I was first forced to travel those deep valleys of despair.

Giving up my freedom in my thirties and watching my father die a few inches everyday was one of the hardest things that I have ever done...without exception! It changed me forever.

My father passed away six months later, on Father's Day...and was buried on my birthday. I think it was symbolic that a great dad passed away on a day set aside to celebrate fatherhood and my consistent prayer for dad to be set free from his suffering was answered on my birthday. When my dad left this world, he knew that he was loved by his only daughter. I did get it right.

When I think about it, I am the original creation of my father, the same as any canvas or story. My father's love and the examples he set while I was growing up have imprinted my life with the same act of creation as any painting or any story.

The canvas of my life and the story of my future are added to daily, but my beginning was started by the bold brush strokes of my wonderful father and the prose of my story was first told by the man that gave me life.

Thanks to the love of my father and the way he lived his life, everyday I do my best...to get it right.

Sun Kitty

By L. J. Shook

Sun Kitty, alias Marmalade, alias Yellow Tiger, alias Fred was the neighbor's cat that came to visit our house once a week or so. Sun Kitty's presence was too big for just one name and only one owner. His air of confidence and strong alpha male attitude was pronounced with every step he took. His large frame and muscular body were ragged around the edges with scabs on his ears and scars from all the Tom-Cat fights he practiced nightly on other male cats that dared to step foot on this claimed turf.

If we had lived in a city, then I'm sure that he would have been a notorious alley cat, but we lived in the country where the homes were a quarter to half mile apart. To be the master of our neighborhood was no small feat. Sun Kitty was master of his domain which included our house where my husband and I lived with our three kids on Cool Lake Road.

Actually, I think the whole neighborhood, in a three-mile radius, was Sun Kitty's territory. He visited the neighbors on rotating bases that only he knew. At each place he was given something to eat and invited in for a stay. And at each place he had a different name that he answered to, the reason for all his aliases. Only one neighbor could claim ownership to Sun Kitty, because he was a free spirit that didn't like to be limited to one person or one place.

On warm summer days he would sit outside the front door and meow in his deep cat voice that sounded like a baby crying and the kids would all come flying out the door with squeals of joy to pet, feed and pamper him. Sun Kitty would relax on the pink doll blanket and pillow, provided by my youngest daughter, and enjoy the food that was hand fed to him with all the royal attitude of a King being waited on by servants.

Sometimes he would let the kids pull him around the yard in their red wagon over-flowing with pillows and blankets. What a sight the old notch-eared cat would be wearing doll dresses put on him by my youngest daughter, who loved him the most. Still intact would be his male, kingly, attitude not dented one bit my wearing a doll dress or bonnet.

Sun Kitty, as he was named by my youngest daughter, because of his yellow fur, loved my kids as much as they loved him. His visits were random and rare, but it was always a joy when he came to stay for a day.

As life went on the kids got bigger and Sun Kitty got older, and the visits grew farther apart until inevitably one summer he didn't come around anymore. We never knew for sure what happened to our beloved visitor, but we were all saddened by the void of not having Sun Kitty in our lives.

My adult children have children and cats of their own, but the mention of Sun Kitty still brings a smile to their lips and a nice memory of their childhood they will always remember.

The Alley Cat

By L. J. Shook

I once was told a story by a social worker regarding a cat she found in the alley on a rainy cold night outside the back door of our Hospice office. This was a likeable older cat with an established lifestyle that rubbed her leg and begged for a little attention, but mostly food. He had a need to be petted and loved, even if only for a minute. I think about the many times in my life that I have been a little lonely like the Farrow Cat and wanted attention and a little love, even for only a minute. I think we have all been there, in lots of ways and for many reasons, in our lifetime, even when we aren't Farrow Cats.

This social worker, being a good-hearted woman, picked up the stray cat and put him in her car, deciding to give him a good home. At first the alley cat soaked up all the attention and good food that was always available, but soon discovered that the rich new food bothered his stomach and sometimes made him sick which caused his new owner to yell at him.

His first crime he remembers was digging food out from the waste basket and garbage can that was more to his liking. A life-long habit of garbage food couldn't be replaced by store bought food from a can, regardless of how expensive it is. He didn't understand why he was getting whacked with a newspaper when all he was doing was what he had done his whole life to survive.

Then the realization that he would no longer get to go outside because he might get fleas, came with baths, medication and the fancy, sissy collar that chaffed his neck and he couldn't get off. He could only dream of the freedom he used to have and all his old friends and haunts he was used to visiting.

His second crime was his routine of spraying the house and

furniture to mark his territory. The repercussion of this routine, that he had always done and had been vital to his survival, was met with a visit to the vets to have surgery so he could no longer spray or have the urge to visit his female friends.

Recovery took a couple of weeks but his lack of any connection to the friends and the lifestyle he had always known caused him to have built up feelings that he worked out by scratching on the furniture. His fourth crime resulted in another trip to the vet to have his claws removed and this trip was even more painful than the first surgery and the recovery even longer.

Now a few months later the relocated Farrow Alley Cat is thinking about living in his new home, with all its limitations and restrictions. He hasn't been happy in months. This caused him to miss his freedom, and that sorrow was stronger than all the petting and love his new owner showered on him. Sick-at-heart for his free life and all that he knew.

In the bay window the alley cat sees a sad reflection of himself, washed clean with a fancy collar, well fed, and miserable. The big window is where he lays for long lonely hours grieving for the life he once had. He has started a new routine of crying out for his friends or even another cat that would listen to his broken heart, his fifth crime. The kind-hearted woman couldn't stand the constant caterwauling, but the farrow cat is not able to be returned to the alley now because he doesn't have claws to hunt or defend himself. So, she takes the cat to the vet, yet again, this time to have his voice box removed so he can no longer make a sound. The vet tried to talk her out of her decision but to no avail so the surgery is done with the stipulation that he would never do another thing to that poor cat.

I didn't know how long the cat lived. I can't imagine he would want to live much longer under such conditions.

This is a true story told to me by a person I once worked with, a generally kind-hearted woman who is sadly out of touch with God's love and only understands and functions in the way worldly love works. I write this with a slant to the cat's point of view and not hers. I still find this story disturbing each time I think of it.

What do you think is the better solution, a shorter life for the cold alley cat with fleas and hunger or a prolonged life with food, comfort and a broken heart?

So many times, I have felt this kind of story has been played out before in our society in the way we treat people of different races, ethnic groups, colors, religions, and cultures where anyone with their own traditions that don't match what some Americans calls their norm. And like the Alley cat something is always lost when forcing another person's life to fit into such a strict, one-of-a-kind, mold of thinking with total disregard for another's happiness or inherited culture.

The Greatest of These Is Love

Oak leaves hang tight as the cold wind blows.
The wind chill bites fingers and toes.
Clouds bring memories of last year's snow.
And colors flicker as Christmas lights glow.
The year has been hard, and faces are pinched,
Shoppers struggle, to not become Grinch.
The war of life is depressing and the economy stinks.
People look tired from loss of winks.
Gas prices rise and the cost of groceries soar.
Everyone's budget is stretched more and more.
What can we do to get out of this mess?
Maybe that is our true...Christmas Test?
Christmas has a way of changing our minds,
Showing us all it is the season to be kind.
When the spirit moves us it is hard to resist,
Christ taught us Love and all that consists.
Take one minute and pull a memory from your past,
Of Christmas love that still lingers and lasts.
Remember the smells and those feelings of bliss,
And how it warms your soul like an Angel's kiss.
Gather close to family and your friends.
And know above all else that Love ascends.
"The Greatest of These is Love," said the Son.
We are not separate, but united as one.
Have a Merry Christmas for another year.
And remember that I hold you close and dear.
The blessing of you...lingers in my thoughts each day.
My prayer is always that, "God light your way."

By L. J. Shook

The Hands That Lifted Charlie

By L. J. Shook

Darkness closed another day at the Group Home. As Case Manager for the mentally handicapped it was hard to maintain a professional distance with my seven adult clients. We shared stories and life experiences about family and work. My job was to listen to their problems, concerns and dreams and guide them into using their best judgement and performing to the best of their ability. My clients were adults and self-sufficient in personal hygiene and doing their laundry. They just needed reminders about taking their med, support when cooking their meals and counseling on how to deal with the world and the people in it.

The client next to me was a thirty-year-old Mildly Mentally Handicapped male who was Bipolar. Charlie had been watching a TV program where angels saved the main character of the movie. After the show was over, he asked me if I believed in Angels. A smile warmed my face, and I answered, "Yes Charlie, I believe in Angels." Then I ask my own question, "How about you? Do you believe in Angels?"

His speech came from a round face, framed by short brown hair with bright blue eyes his words came out in a rush with excitement. Charlie was a rocker and would sit and rock for hours, back and forth. In his familiar swaying position, he stumbled over his words, but slowly the story of how he came to believe in Angles unfolded.

Charlie's story started when he was eleven. He had been playing with other children around a train trestle that stood very tall at the end of his street. He told how he was showing off and trying to fit in with the other kids, the boys dared him to climb to the top of the train trestle. He quietly told me how he climbed up to the top of the train trestle, lost his footing and fell.

Large eyes looked at me in earnest as he rocked back and forth. "Do you know when I was falling, I felt hands under me? The hands caught me and moved me sideways." Excitement shone from Charlie's face as he pulled up his pant leg and pushed down his sock to show a large, red, jagged scar on his right ankle. He said, "I bumped my head too, but I didn't get hurt bad at all.

When I fell, I went straight down where the cement blocks were piled up on the ground. But I didn't land on the blocks because the hands caught me and moved me sideways. The firemen who helped me said I would be dead if I had landed on the cement blocks."

With a radiant smile he said, "I think those hands were Angel hands and they saved my life. So, I feel I am supposed to tell this story. After my fall I started to believe in Angels."

I asked Charlie, "Why did you still hurt your leg bad enough to leave a scar?" Charlie smiled and said, "That's simple, the scar was God's permanent way of reminding me and what happened wasn't a good thing, this way when I see the scar I can remember not do something like that again."

The pureness of that moment brought tears to my eyes and a lump to my throat. I knew without a doubt that Charlie fully understood the story he was telling and had spoken the truth. Warmth filled my heart and with joy and gratitude as I whispered, "Thank You", to the hands that lifted our Charlie."

Third Shift Blues

By L. J. Shook

My body drags home after eight hours of standing,
Everything hurts and sleep is demanding.

Outside the strong wind, swirls, and tree leaves rattle.
My attempt to watch the morning news sounds like prattle.

The active noise of day strengthens, as I go to bed,
but my body is desperate for the reverse instead.

Thoughts come and go, and rest can barely be grasped.
my mind craves sleep, not this restless nap.

Another day used, abused and gone,
My mind tallies all my rights and wrongs.

The light came early today and went home late.
How many hours can you force a day to take?

My eyes are bleary, and my lips form a pout.
Mind chatter wrestles my calm, and I want to shout.

Such is the life of the third shift crew.
My body clock keeps ticking but is all askew.

I'm always tired and never quite awake.
The sleepy man's shuffle is my feet's only break.

Such are the woes of the job market these days.
You take what you can find and adjust to its ways.

Toad Kissing

By L. J. Shook

When I was young and very small,
My father read me stories, fairytales and all.

One story told of a prince turned into a frog,
by a wicked witch that lived near a bog.

The prince needed a kiss to break the spell.
About the witch's terrible deed, he could not tell.

A beautiful princess with hair long and fair,
was to kiss the green frog, with nary a care.

It all sounded good, it seemed to make sense.
Just kiss a frog and get a prince.

Years long after that innocent day,
I sit and wonder with much dismay.

How many kissed toads does it take,
to change a frog and the prince to wake?

My best friend listened to a sorrowful tale,
About my last date and all it curtailed.

She too was a toad-kisser from way back,
and understood my query and state of lack.

Her words of wisdom were the very same,
that I had heard before, and she always claims.

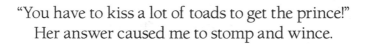

"You have to kiss a lot of toads to get the prince!"
Her answer caused me to stomp and wince.

Kissing toad after toad and frog after frog,
had my head in a spin and my mind all clogged.

How many? Just how many kissed toads does it take,
to reach my toad-kissing quota and a prince to wake?

My lips are turning green, and my voice has a croak.
I'm starting to think this whole thing is a bad hoax!

Was I told wrong and lead astray?
Misinformation has caused too many women much delay.

Childhood fables have damaged young girls' minds.
A different idea is what's needed for this day and time.

Too many lost dreams were wasted on getting the prince.
Making another person responsible doesn't make sense.

New thoughts have become my best tool,
I don't need a prince to make me cool.

I am beautiful, strong, empowered and so much more,
My life is what I make it, with opportunities galore.

So, love, dance, be happy and embrace life's bliss,
forget **catching** the prince and just enjoy the kiss.

Tood and Luke

By L.J Shook

When I was little, I used to go fishing with my dad at the neighbor's house a couple of miles down the road. Luke had some land that he farmed out but down a long dirt path behind the barn and field past the woods was a large pond hidden by trees. Luke only let a few people he liked fish at his pond so very few people knew about it.

Luke and his wife Tood were an old catholic couple and at six I thought they were biblically old people, the kind they talked about in Grandma's Sunday school class old. Luke was bowed legged and walked with a cane and Tood was real pretty in a wrinkly kind of way and had flat hair with big waves. She was wearing a flowery dress and ugly shoes. They never had kids of their own and only a few distant family members, so my parents would take them to doctor appointments and do things for them.

One day my mother took me to their house for them to watch me. I had Shirley Temple curls, a full dress that I could twirl around in and a tooth missing in front. I think my mother thought they could handle me for a short time. When looking back I'm not sure who was watching who.

They had no toys, no understanding of kids and no skills to cope with a six-year-old. I was left in the house with Tood, and to me their house had strange furniture, strange food, and strange smells. I asked Tood why she had a picture of Jesus on the wall, why she had a necklace with a cross, and how did she get those holes in her ears and those pretty, gold things, hanging down? In short order I was sent outside to play with Luke.

Luke spent his days sitting in his old rusty chair so I explored the driveway with the funny-looking rocks that resembled snails and fossils, but at six you can only play with rocks for so long. When the fun ran out with the rocks I went to talk to Luke. He sat in a funny old metal chair that tipped back without falling and he was spitting brown stuff out of his mouth. I asked him what he was doing, and he told me he was chewing tobacco. He caught a grasshopper and squeezed it, and brown stuff came out of the bug's mouth. He said it chewed tobacco too. It has to be okay if bugs were doing it.

I asked him if I could see so he opened his mouth to show me, and dark juicy stuff trickled out of the corners of his mouth. I was fascinated. He was an old man proud of his skill and he pointed to a dandelion, spit and hit it in middle. Now that was a neat trick, a lot more fun than driveway rocks. So, I asked Luke if he would teach me how to spit. He gave me instructions, but I didn't have enough wet stuff in my mouth to hit anything. So, I asked Luke if he would give me some of that brown stuff so I could spit like him. Of course, he refused and told me that would upset my mother.

Poor Luke, he just wasn't prepared to deal with my toothless smile and my Shirley Temple curls. After I said, "Please Mr. Luke," and pulled on his arm he gave in and handed me a small brown piece that sort of looked like dog poop, but it smelled okay, so I plopped it in my mouth.

It tasted horrible and was a little bit hot. Luke said to chew it and make it gooey so I could spit. Within a few minutes I was able to spit at dandelions just like Luke. My missing tooth in front created a problem because some of the brown juice would slip out and go down my chin but also slipped down my throat and into my stomach.

At six... I had taken my first step on the wild side. I had used my curls to sweet talk a man out of his tobacco and learned to chew and spit. When my mom arrived, there was brown goo running down my chin and I was three shades of green and ready to up chuck all the tobacco juice that had slid down my throat into my tummy.

Mom yelled at poor Mr. Luke. When I look back at the whole thing, I feel sorry for Mr. Luke, he didn't have a chance to come out of that situation without being in trouble. He was up against little girl curls, a toothless smile, a dress that twirls and a little girl who could sweetly talk him out of his chew.

Twinkle of Color

Twinkles of color, and tree's brilliant glow,
Boughs stretched wide with presents below.
A scent of pine and majestic stance,
draws me close, for a better glance.
Ornaments sparkle on the holiday tree,
Oh, the beauty... my wondrous glee.
Christmas music vibrates along my spine.
Written lyrics, dance in half-beat time.
The urge to bake has overcome my senses,
creating fancy treats and culinary pretenses.
A candle's glow illuminates and wins,
comfort brought to the room's shadowy tinge.
Oh, celebrated season and holiday pride
You have chased away my depression tide.
The color red dresses up the season,
Cheery thoughts embrace winter's teasing.
Hard snow on the ground sounds gives a crunch
White flakes deliver a wintry punch.
Bells that jingle and church bells that ring
Harold Christmas and all that it brings
The reason for the holiday reminds me to care
And lifts my thoughts from life's ordinary despair
Thank you Kind Spirit for the wonderful lift,
And a Loving Son's forever spiritual gift.

By L. J. Shook

What a Difference a Dream Can Make

By L. J. Shook

Have you ever wondered where that special spark comes from that causes one person to be an Olympic Champion and another to become a Criminal? In the DVD, "The Secret," Dr. Dennis Waitly talks about how he brought creative visualization (visual motor rehearsal) to the Olympics program from the Apollo Space program. When athletes were hooked up to bio-feed-back equipment and ran their event in their mind all the same muscles and parts of the brain fired up in the same way as if they were performing their event. The mind couldn't tell the difference between the actual event and the visual event.

What if this same theory applied to a person having a dream? Not the night-time sort of dream but the sort of dream that is a vision or goal of what you want to do or become during your life? An Olympic Champion seems to have a well-defined dream that has been recognized early, encouraged and supported by family, friends and teachers. Not one child, when asked about their dreams, has ever said to me, "I want to be a criminal or someone who grows up to buy and sell drugs and do bad things to hurt other people and myself." Our jails are overflowing and bulging with lost dreams. Maybe the difference between a criminal and an Olympic athlete is their ability to follow their dream?

Usually, a child will dream of doing heroic deeds, fighting the monsters of the night and the bad guys of the day. It's only after hope and dreams are lost or altered by abuse, or forgotten by adults in their lives, that a child loses that spark called a dream.

Even without abuse and neglect there will always be a group of people to tell you that your dream can't be done, or you are wasting your time. The pressure to conform to the mass of mediocrity thinking people will always be present.

Can you imagine the effect we could have on our future and the future of our children by recognizing a dream in one child, one teen, or even one adult and helping them to believe in their dreams? Our dreams don't have to make money or bring fame. Just having a dream brings back our spark and divine essence. That spark can change a person and affect the whole world.

Surviving the moment plays such a big part in raising children that sometimes we forget, as parents, how important it is to believe in the future, and our dreams for the future. Paying the bills, working long hours, feeding and clothing our children and providing shelter takes a huge toll on our lives. In the chaos of living, we forget to dream, and we forget to teach our children to dream. If we don't teach our children how important it is to have dreams for their future, then who will? A child may change their dream a hundred times before they become an adult but that doesn't matter. It's not the result of a dream but the act of dreaming that keeps the creative spark of love alive.

My dad was a wonderful loving man, and I couldn't have asked for a better father. But he never once asked me what my dreams were for the future. I don't think he ever knew my dreams. I think he had dreams of his own because he painted beautiful pictures of the Wild West, but he never talked about his dreams or asked me about mine. It was always assumed that I would get a job, marry, and have children. But for me those weren't dreams they were just assumed duties that girls my age was expected to do.

When I was a senior in high school I wanted to join the Peace Corps after graduation. The signature of my parents was required on the forms. My dreams weren't taken seriously, and even ridiculed by my mother. After that I didn't share my dreams so I would never be vulnerable again. After a while I quit believing that dreams could come true, and I went on to do the duties that girls my age have always done.

Secretly I still had dreams, but they were buried deep. In their place I had wishes like, "I wish I would win the lottery. I wish I had a new car. I wish I had a new job or had more money." Deep soul dreams were covered over by shallow surface wishes. People didn't make fun of you when you had wishes. How could I have dreams, that would require believing in myself, and that had not been taught to me nor something that I understood or ever experienced.

A few years later, while working at a Radio Station, part of my job was to schedule speakers for our call-in program. While planning and talking to the speaker for the next day's program he asked me some personal questions about myself and my dreams. There was hesitation on my part about sharing such a vulnerable part of myself, but he had a nice voice and was three thousand miles away. I thought that I would never meet this person, so it was easy to tell my long-ignored dreams to a stranger on the phone.

Total surprise came when he gave encouragement to me and value to my thoughts and dreams. He even spoke in such a matter that caused me to believe that dreams were an important part of living, necessary even. This nice man I now call my mentor has continued to encourage me with phone calls and his wisdom for the past twenty years. He was a total stranger that changed my life because he took the time to encourage my dreams. His act of, "giving me back my dreams," has been one of my greatest and longest lasting gifts during my life.

Regardless of your age it is never too late to start dreaming. There isn't a day that passes when an opportunity doesn't present itself to believe in your own ability or someone else's. If all we can give is one word of encouragement to another or an opportunity to believe each day there is a possibility for something wonderful to happen, then that can be enough to make a difference.

One of my dreams was to be a writer and another was to paint wonderful pictures. Since I started following my dreams again several of my stories have been published and I was even an editor of a magazine for beginning writers. I hang my ribbons that I have won next to the pictures that I painted and entered in local art contests. I don't have fame or fortune from following my dreams, but I am truly richer because of the experience.

My seven-year-old grandson shares my love of art and by my side painted a buffalo and won Grand Champion for his painting. His picture and name were on the front page of the local newspaper.

All that I ask you to do is stop and think about your dreams and if you don't have a dream then find one, or just remember. Ask other people what they dream. Because without dreams we wouldn't have music, art, movies, books or trips to the moon. Just stop and think of all the things we have and live with daily that required a dream to make it happen. Everything in our world once started with a dream.

My catcher of dreams didn't enter my life until after my children were almost raised. I, like my parents before me, hadn't taught my children about dreams. How can you teach something that you do not know about yourself? But it's never too late to make a change, and never, never too late to have dreams. Today my adult children and grandchildren share our dreams, believe in each other, and give constant encouragement.

In doing the things you love you demonstrate courage, self-respect, self-worth, and set an example for others to follow. All of us can remember having dreams sometime in our lives. If we were lucky, we followed our dreams, but others may have lost their dreams along the way. Wouldn't it be nice to help someone find their lost dreams again or teach the wonderful gift of having a dream to a child, especially a child you love?

A dream standing alone, without action, is not enough to see it fulfilled but a dream that has been loved can put light in the world. Thomas Edison's dream gave light to the world. Our dream may not light the world, but it could be that spark that would give us something to look forward to...plan for...live for...die for. Without dreams life loses its joy, its passion, and its reason to continue. A life too long without dreams needs illness, medication, alcohol, drugs, or violence to cover up the pain of not being heard. Dreaming is the difference between living and existing. A person can never get too old or be too young to have dreams.

Our country was built on dreams and catching dreams. If we all had a goal to stop and catch a dream or two for ourselves and someone else, what a huge, long-lasting gift that would be. If you have forgotten your dreams, then just take a minute and... remember or make a new dream.

I know for sure you can change a life, alter a family and make a difference with every dream you... catch.

When I'm an Ole Woman

By L J Shook

When I'm an old woman and live with my kids,
They'll be so excited, and they will all take bids,
Excited on who gets the ole' girl with her quirks,
They will be delighted with the extra burden of work.
I will do all their childhood behavior as best as I can.
I will fight, argue, and yell with mutinous stand.
I'll run naked in the garden and dance in the sun,
It will make them crazy, and it will be so much fun.
I'll throw my clothes on the bed, the chair and the floor,
And make sure the laundry basket over-flows with more.
I'll climb out the window and jump from the roof.
I'll scare the puddin' right out of their stuff.
I'll work in their garden and hoe off the beans,
Throw vegetables at them and make them scream.
I'll hog the toys, swing, and bike and I'll not share,
They will shake their heads with a look of despair.
When I am eating dinner I will argue about my food,
like peas, beans and sprouts and anything stewed.
I will leave my knitting needles all lying about
Until they trip, limp and start to shout.
I will smear catsup on my arm when it's time to do dishes,
pretending I'm wounded, so I can't follow their wishes.
I'll hotrod my motorcycle until I bounce off the fence,
Then cry and milk the hurt with hours of pretense.
I'll throw cat turds from the sand pile and
rotten tomatoes from the garden,
and be as disruptive as I can be and never ask their pardon.
I will gag on my food and pretend I can't eat
Until they offer dessert or something sweet.

I will whine and cry and constantly shout.
Until they think their minds are going to fall out.
I will make cracks about their getting
old, and losing their sight,
And grin when they must repeat something to get it right.
Then I will give them my look of sweetness and light,
And frequently remind them about being so uptight.
Or I will run off four baby-sitters in a short period of time.
And make them all crazy and start to drool and whine.
Next I will have cuts, scrapes, bruises, stitches and more.
The road will have groves straight to the hospital door.
When my kid's hair falls out or it starts to turn gray,
Then I'll know I have done my best during my stay.
Oh, those pay backs are hard...as they surely must be,
Remember grandchildren all fall from that same family tree.
It will be their time of passage through the middle-age stage,
between children and parents... to wise old sage.

When The Music Ends

By L. J. Shook

We have heard it said that you could never go back, and that is true if you are expecting everything to be the same. But I think there are times we need to revisit old friends, old haunts, and even old situations and in doing so it causes us to gauge the distance we have grown, matured or have come away from old patterns that no longer work for us. Such was the case for me.

One of the first impressions that I encountered, during a visit back to Cincinnati was that so many times we view life through a microscope and not a telescope. Cincinnati was where I went to get away from my family's dysfunction and find my future. I spent ten glorious years escaping and recreating the only true material that I must work with... me. When I had finished my reconstruction, it was time for me to move back to be closer to my grandbabies.

During one of my visits back to Cincinnati the first person on my list to visit was a client I had during my time in the healthcare profession. His name is Harrison, and regardless of whether it was by design (God's design) or choice, he was a part of my life while I lived there. Harrison was someone I put to bed on weekends, for three years.

Harrison is a quadriplegic, a world class athlete, who was trying out for the Olympics in Kick Boxing and during a competition was kicked by a competitor that broke his back, fifth vertebrae down. He has been in a wheelchair since he was thirty. I would spend one paid hour putting Harrison to bed and another unpaid hour talking to him. Harrison lived with his mother and was a wheelchair-bound shut-in by circumstance.

The only things from the outside world that came into Harrison's life were brought in by friends, TV, family, or the nurses and health care workers that came to care for him. We checked his vitals, bathed him, shaved him, prepared his meals, and got him up in the morning and put him to bed at night. Most of his ideas and images of life, for the past ten years, have been filtered through other people's perspectives and limitations or the slanted views of TV.

Harrison had charm, looks and a highly developed skill of pushing people's buttons that he learned during his years of competing in sports, but now used on all who enter his domain. At first, I thought it was a man thing, but soon came to realize this was his way of feeling like he had some power over something. When you have no control over your legs, hands, or bowels and can barely feed yourself, and your whole life is dependent on someone else, you crave to have some power over something. It was a two-fold blessing, by pushing buttons Harrison viewed real people, real emotions and heard real-life troubles in place of the prefabricated, canned version of life that he viewed with his movies and TV.

My first couple of months helping Harrison was a profound and irritating experience. I was touched, as were all the caregivers who passed through his door, with his kind eyes and the accepting nature of his plight. But I soon learned that if Harrison was pushing your buttons and had you reacting, he was not in danger of being asked questions he did not want to answer or of you discovering what was really going on inside. Harrison was hiding out so he could make it through each day. Until I came along everyone else was willing to use Harrison like a free therapist, dumping all their cares and woes on him while they administered to his needs, he would give his bed-bound therapy and say a prayer or two for each person and all would appear happy.

The problem was it created an even lonelier existence for Harrison than he already had. I wanted to know the real Harrison. I challenged his views on religion, family, friends, politics, the world, and most of all, on himself and he eagerly challenged mine. His wounded soul would cringe a little with my prodding, but the competitive athlete would take over and the duel would begin.

All the perimeters that the world used to define us as people fell away, it didn't matter that I was a woman and he was a man, that I could walk, and he could not. It was not important that I was seventeen years older, nor that he was black, and I was white. None of the definitions that would affect a relationship in the outside world existed during the time I spent being a caregiver to Harrison. Even the definition of relationship did not apply. We were just two people sharing a friendship on our own journey of self-discovery at a spiritual level which means that you really understand each other.

The blessing of this kind of relationship is that you meet a person on a soul level. Most relationships only touch the surface, this kind of relationship is usually the norm, but deep down inside there is always a craving that at least one person in the world will care enough to truly get you.

The downside to this kind of friendship is that once you find that kind of person you never want to let go, it becomes a crutch to lean on during those times when life has knocked you down. We are so rarely understood and that creates a need seldom filled in our day-to-day world. When you are understood on so many levels and the relationship is altered, as in my case I moved away, then the void is felt at a more profound level. For me it felt like the death of a friend. My experience with Harrison helped me to embrace life more openly with everyone I met. This was only possible because of the way Harrison's life and circumstances had touched my life and heart.

Harrison on the other hand did not fare so well. He didn't have the freedom or the ability to go and find new people with like thinking. Shortly before I moved away, Harrison's mother passed away. So, I am sure the death of his beloved mother and my moving was like a double loss for him. I stayed in contact and Harrison moved around a lot, living first with one brother then another and another. Every few months I would go back to Cincinnati to visit friends and check on Harrison, but as my life in Indiana expanded the time grew longer between visits. I asked a friend to check in on Harrison and keep me informed.

On one visit I picked up my Cincinnati friend, and we went to visit Harrison together. A phone conversation a few months earlier had Harrison excited with the anticipation of him moving into a new apartment with his brother. The call did not prepare me for what my friend and I would find. The apartment was new and genuinely nice, the furniture attractive and the rooms beautifully decorated but the condition of Harrison was shocking. My friend Harrison had long hair, a beard, unkempt fingernails, and had lost 40 or 50 pounds. His toenails had grown so long that they curled back under the end of his toes. He had not eaten regularly or been bathed in quite a while. The odor of neglect hung heavily in the air. He now had a bed sore from never leaving his bed and his brother, who was the person responsible for caring for him was a truck driver and had not been home in a couple of weeks.

Harrison's eyes were hollowed out, his face drawn, and he had a raging urinary tract infection. His brother had canceled his home care agency and messed up his Medicare, so Harrison was no longer eligible to receive help.

My good friend and I went to work on Harrison and his apartment. She brought in food, cooked him a meal, laundered his clothes and bedding, and put his home in order. My work on Harrison involved bathing, shaving, trimming his hair and nails, changing the bed linen, and nursing his physical needs, the whole-time tears choking my throat. My friend and I managed to put Harrison's 6ft 2in frame in his wheelchair for a while, so we could clean and change his bed, but it was hard on him sitting up when he had not done it for so long and he passed out. Finally, we finished all our tasks, Harrison was clean, fed, doctored, loved, and put back to bed. We had done all we could to the best of our ability.

During the six hours we spent with Harrison I called the home health care agency I had worked for, when I first met Harrison, trying to get him some service. We called friends, family members, and even asked neighbors to see if they would help him. I did manage to get one of his old nurses to come and check his bed sores, urinary tract infection and do a bowel treatment on her own time without pay. Every avenue that we pursued in trying to get Harrison help was blocked, as if higher powers were purposely closing off all options. My friend and I left Harrison's apartment despondent and crying.

I had a serious talk with Harrison before I left his apartment. We discussed how no one was taking care of his needs. He is a forty-year-old man, a survivor, and I was not his mother, wife or even his care giver who was I to tell him what to do. We talked about what was best for him, but he would be the one that had to decide. All our phone calls had educated us both enough to know that would be his only hope. Harrison had one option which would provide him with daily healthcare, but that would require him to go into a nursing home for a period of time to get his Medicare reestablished. It was going to be impossible for him to keep living in the apartment alone without it and it would be his responsibility to call the nursing home if that was his decision.

After we left, I took my good friend to her home in Cincinnati before heading back to Indiana. You know you have a great friend when she works shoulder to shoulder with you when someone is in need. I barely remember the two and half hours it took to drive back. I was praying and crying the entire way home. Harrison was such a man of God reading his bible for hours each day. I could not understand how God could desert this man in his time of need. I remember asking God that question and the answer I received was surprising. God told me to be still in my spirit, all is well. This was a time for Harrison to decide whether he wanted to die and be done with it all and come home or continue to live with all his limitations here on earth. This was Harrison's time to decide, and everything was in place for whatever his choice would be.

A couple of days later I called and received information that he was on his way to a nursing home, he had made his decision. My thoughts were sad and happy at the same time. I was thrilled that my friend had made the choice to live but deep inside I was troubled with what this kind of change would do to Harrison's spirit.

A year later I sat next to Harrison in the guest lobby of the nursing home. He is back to pushing buttons, being arrogant and the old routines he used when we first met. His survival instinct is locked and loaded in place and his attitude makes me sad. I see his regression and ask myself who I am to judge whether this is good or bad, I cannot comprehend what he must endure each day to make it through living in a nursing home at the age of forty-one, with all the limitations of the older people living around him.

A half an hour of his, "Old Button-Pushing Routine," is about all that I can manage, and I said to him, "In another minute I'm going to smack you." Without the need for an explanation, he knew exactly what I meant. I told him I thought I had gotten the wrong man from his room, and I was going to wheel him back and get the other guy because he must be the real Harrison. A flicker of my old friend looked at me with a slight grin and I knew somewhere he was still in there, buried deep to avoid the pain of his life. My spirit aches for him. Part of me wonders if he made the right decision a year ago, in choosing to live. Only Harrison and God know the answer to that question.

I don't know Harrison's purpose for coming to earth, and we all have one, or how his being paralyzed affects his life's journey. Regardless of his life purpose, being a person who cares for his welfare and his happiness makes it painful to watch. Maybe that is Harrison's purpose in life, to help us to remember love, compassion, patience, and understanding in our spirit, for all the people around us. If the time comes when we no longer find it painful to watch the struggles of the Harrisons in this world then we will know we have lost our humanity.

Which is better... to starve to death physically and be done with it or to slowly starve emotionally and suffer spiritually? My old friend and I exchanged a few challenges, but I hold back, knowing that it is unfair of me to draw out the real Harrison and open him up to being vulnerable again when I will be leaving in a few minutes.

Sadness weighs down my heart and the guilt of leaving him bothers me. Our paths were only meant to cross for a while and now it is time for me to walk away.

My trip back to Indiana was spent in conversation with a good friend, who traveled to Cincinnati with me. She is a social worker with Veterans Hospital, and she cares for the Harrisons of this world all day in her job. I asked her how she handles it, caring for them and then walking away with so many of their needs still unmet.

Her answer is as wise as she is, and she said, "You can only dance with one person at a time, dance your best dance possible but when the music ends your dance is over and you must walk away."

The music for Harrison and I is now at an end. It is time for us to go our separate ways. I wish him happiness, good health, and love to surround him for the rest of his days.

The best love you can give to another is not to boss them, judge them, control them, nurture them to the point of suffocation, or cripple their thinking, but to give care when needed and love them enough to let them decide when they are strong enough to fly.

I will be forever thankful to have met Harrison and cherish the lessons I learned during the time our lives crossed paths.

Writer's Block

By L. J. Shook

Do you have pen in hand, ready to write,
Do you write day and night?
Are your words taking flight?
Do your verbs pound the ground,
In poems and stories piled around.
Do you write pages filled with prose,
Or hide out and pick your toes?
Do your puns spin and turn
Or fall to earth and slowly burn?
Do your adjectives love your nouns?
Or do they stink and cause a frown?
Can you write a line or quip,
Or are you blocked and want to quit?

You Have Loved Well Poem

By L. J. Shook

We go through our day
tripping over our mistakes,
bumping into bad habits,
and trying to outrun bad decisions,
and by the end of the day, we sometimes
wonder if we have done anything right.
We are human, flawed and God's
beautiful work in progress.
I just wanted you to know
that you have lifted us all to a new level
by watching your loving care.
Thank you for the privilege of learning
from your wondrous gift of love.
You did it right.
You have loved well
and blessed everyone around you
by showing us all how to love unconditionally.
Thank you for your
courage in making a difference.

Printed in the United States
by Baker & Taylor Publisher Services